1971

STUDIES IN ROMANCE LANGUAGES: 4

CHRISTIAN ALLEGORY
IN EARLY HISPANIC POETRY

CHRISTIAN ALLEGORY

IN EARLY HISPANIC POETRY

DAVID WILLIAM FOSTER

THE UNIVERSITY PRESS OF KENTUCKY

LEXINGTON

STANDARD BOOK NUMBER 8131-1230-3
LIBRARY OF CONGRESS CATALOG NUMBER 76-111508

COPYRIGHT © 1970 BY THE UNIVERSITY PRESS OF KENTUCKY

*A Statewide cooperative scholarly publishing agency
serving Berea College, Centre College of Kentucky,
Eastern Kentucky University, Kentucky State College,
Morehead State University, Murray State University,
University of Kentucky, University of Louisville, and
Western Kentucky University*

EDITORIAL AND SALES OFFICES: LEXINGTON, KENTUCKY 40506

PRINTED IN SPAIN

DEPÓSITO LEGAL: V. 4.857 - 1970

ARTES GRÁFICAS SOLER, S. A. — JÁVEA, 28 — VALENCIA (8) — 1970

Sabé, Nena, que tu amor "está en mí como un poema / que no he logrado detener en palabras."

CONTENTS

PREFACE

This study explores aspects of Christian literary allegory as a recurrent structural motif in premodern literature. An attempt has been made to define that motif and to discuss some of its exemplary realizations in dramatic and lyric poetry. Therefore, emphasis is placed on the analysis and interpretation of a series of carefully selected key texts, and no attempt has been made to write a history of Christian literary allegory in the Peninsula.

Focus is on literature which can broadly be called "medieval." However, due to the scarcity of documents from the pre-Renaissance dramatic tradition, several works from the sixteenth century have been included which can be called neither early nor medieval. In so violating the traditional boundaries I hope to provide a more thorough characterization of the subject than would be possible if the study were limited to the relatively small corpus of pre-1500 texts.

Most of the works considered are in Spanish, but for the period in question any distinction other than simply "Hispanic" is somewhat arbitrary—both Alfonso and Gil Vicente wrote in Castilian and Portuguese. Therefore, works in Castilian, Portuguese, and Catalan are introduced wherever pertinent.

This study was completed under a faculty grant from Arizona State University.

INTRODUCTION

Sabed que Dios ha nacido,
en la ciudad de Belén,
es el Mesias, por quien
serà el hombre redimido,
y alcançara el sumo bien.
Por otro nombre Emanuel,
es el que llamo Mesias
es por quien dize Isaias,
comera manteca y miel
en sus sanctas profecias.
La serpiente que Moysen
ante todos leuantò,
a mi Dios significo
y el hara en Hierusalem
lo que alli se figurò.

(Pedro Suárez de Robles,
*Danza del Santissimo Nas-
cimento* vv. 6-20)

THE TERM *allegory* has multiple applications. Within literary and biblical scholarship and in the writings of the medieval authors, three usages are found: (1) Greek or Hellenistic allegory, where the sign is important only for what is signified, (2) one of the three nonliteral meanings of biblical exegesis, the formal level dealing with the events in the New Testament and their relation to the Old Testament, as opposed to the moral or tropological and the anagogical or eschatalogical levels, (3) the nonliteral meaning of biblical exegesis or Christian figural interpretation, as opposed to the literal or historical meaning of the sign.

There is abundant scholarship dealing with the first and most general usage of the word *allegory* and extensive opinion concerning the relationship between the fourfold way of biblical interpretation and imaginative literature, [1] but a nonscriptural understanding of the terms *Christian figural allegory* and *figural interpretation* is relatively recent. Consequently, few medieval poetry studies attempt to demonstrate how many of the works traditionally grouped as allegory lie beyond classical practices. This study comments on several major Hispanic works which exemplify Christian figural allegory as a system of allusive symbolism or as a structural design radically at variance with the practices of Hellenistic allegory.

Hellenistic allegory is one of the most significant legacies of classical antiquity to western literature. A cursory examination of the vast body of texts in the Latin, Romance, and German vernaculars reveals that from the earliest fragments to the mature works of the High Middle Ages, and with increasing intensity in Renaissance, baroque, neo-Classical and modern literature, Hellenistic allegory has enjoyed an imposing prestige.

The dominance of allegory in European literature has created a general critical category. However, during the patristic period and the Middle Ages, allegory in the Hellenistic, Platonic sense existed alongside another type of "allegory" sometimes called "symbolic representation." Figural allegory, a concept inherent to the Jewish historical and prophetical interpretation of the Old Testament, had already developed into a disciplined technique for understanding scripture. A dualism between pagan allegory and Jewish figural allegory developed within the Christian culture after the early church fathers adopted figural allegory. [2]

---

[1] There are far too many treatments of the subject to cite here. See in particular Chandler R. Post, *Medieval Spanish Allegory* (Cambridge, Mass., 1915). For recent research on the subject see Angus Fletcher, *Allegory, the Theory of a Symbolic Mode* (Ithaca, N. Y., 1964). Basic Studies are C. S. Lewis, *Allegory of Love* (New York, 1958); and Gilbert Highet, *The Classical Tradition: Greek and Roman Influences on Western Literature* (New York, 1957). There is no one comprehensive study on the subject; see, however, "Allegory," in Alex Preminger, *Encyclopedia of Poetry and Poetics* (Princeton, N. J., 1965), pp. 12-15.

[2] Hellenistic allegory dominated the exegetical writings of the members of the so-called Alexandrian school (Origen is its most important spokesman), who, in their proximity to the sources of classical culture, affirmed that scripture could only be understood in a symbolic sense, while denying any importance attached to the literal meaning of the Word. Such a pro-

A discussion of the literature which resulted from the assimilation of Jewish figural allegory into European culture demands clarification of the concepts "figure" and "figural." Erich Auerbach

---

cedure adhered to the Platonic nature of Hellenistic allegory in its implication that tangible reality is a deceitful shadow of a higher ideal truth. Alexandrian exegesis, therefore, doubted the possibility of any intrinsic truth to be found in the Old Testament and in the other manifestations of the Old pre-Christian Law. All these trappings were but allegories of the Christian revelation.

In terms of the history of the western Church, nevertheless, we know that Jewish allegory as it was espoused by the so-called Antiochian school (cf. St. John Crysostom) emerged the stronger of the two, thanks in great part to the support of their methodology to be found in the extremely influential writings of St. Augustine and St. Thomas Aquinas. Central to the concept of Jewish allegory is the role of existential historical prophecy. The men, places, and events of one moment in history, literal, "real," and intrinsically worthy at that moment, prophesy and prefigure the men, places, and events of the history of mankind to come. For the Jews, that history was essentially one of revelation and becoming, since it was directed toward the Coming of the Messiah, the fulfillment of the covenant, and the restoration of man from his fall. It is common knowledge how Christianity was able, principally through the efforts of St. Paul, to elaborate its promise to mankind within the ready-made historical and visionary framework which it came to adopt in such great detail from Jewish thought and custom. For the importance of Paul and his writings in securing Christianity a historical perspective in relationship to the Jewish tradition, see the excellent summaries of Frederick B. Artz, *The Mind of the Middle Ages,* 3d ed. (New York, 1958), pp. 56-59; and Karl Vossler, *Medieval Culture: An Introduction to Dante and His Times,* trans. William Cranston Lawton (New York, 1958), pp. 36-39. With the firm conviction that the New Law of Christianity fulfilled and supplanted the Old Jewish Law, thus giving a new and more encouraging direction to man's progress toward reunion with his Maker, biblical exegesis as it generally came to be practiced in the West depended in greater and greater measure on the subtle intricacies of Jewish figural allegory. As far as the exegetes of the western Church were concerned, all of the past, both pagan and Jewish, represented literal history which embodied at the same time the prophecy of the higher meaning of the eventual Christian Law and, further, of the ultimate resolution of history in the Last Judgment. Such a "respect" for the validity of the past and such an attention to the complex interrelationships between past, present, and future had a profound effect, not only on the character of the western Church, but eventually on the literature produced within the sphere of influence of that Church as well. See the excellent introduction on the history of Alexandrian and Antiochian exegesis in Johan Chydenius, *The Typological Problem in Dante: A Study in the History of Medieval Ideas* (Helsinki, 1958). See also the indispensable article on "Exegesis (Biblical)," in *The Catholic Encyclopedia* (New York, 1909), pp. 692-706.

defines "figure" as allegory in the largest sense: [3] "Figural interpretation establishes a connection between two events or persons, the first of which signifies not only itself but also the second, while the second encompasses or fulfills the first. ... Since in figural interpretation one thing stands for another, since one thing represents and signifies the other, figural interpretation is allegorical in the widest sense. But it differs from most of the allegorical forms known to us by the historicity both of the sign and what it signifies" (pp. 53-54).

Auerbach feels that a distinction resides in the fact that allegory, i.e., Hellenistic allegory, is often the very mechanical substitution of one sign for another, with the sign having only an extrinsic meaning by virtue of its referent, while figural interpretation seeks to establish a vital and historical relationship between two sets of ocurrences, such as the persons and events of the Old and the New Testaments. As such, figures are historically bound in a way that symbols and allegorical entities are not. Auerbach demonstrates that such a procedure, which he believes appealed more to the masses than the esoteric nature of the Hellenistic literary and Alexandrian exegetical allegories, has direct antecedents in the need of the early church fathers to reconcile and justify a pagan tradition:

Allegory long maintained its position; in the doctrine of the fourfold meaning of Scripture, it wholly determined one of the four meanings, the ethical, and partly accounted for another, the analogical [sic, for "anagogical"]. And yet I believe, though I can offer no strict proof of it, that independently, that is to say, without the support of the figural method, it would have had little influence on the freshly converted peoples. There is something scholarly, indirect, even abstruse about it, except on rare occasions when a mystic breathes force into it. ... Figural phenomenal prophecy, however, had grown out of a definitive historical situation, the Christian break with Judaism and the Christian mission among the Gentiles; it had a historical function.

---

[3] Erich Auerbach, "Figura," in his *Scenes from the Drama of European Literature* (New York, 1959), pp. 11-76. This is a basic treatment of figural interpretation and its relation to allegory. Auerbach traces the concept from antiquity through medieval Latin and Romance literatures, concluding with a discussion of figural interpretation as applied to Dante. With respect to Dante see the study by Chydenius already cited. In passing one might mention that figural (from Latin *figura*) and typological (from Greek *typus*) interpretation are terms which are used interchangeably in discussions of the subject.

Its integral, firmly theological view of history and the providential order of the world gave it the power to capture the imagination and innermost feeling of the convert nations. (pp. 55-56)

The confrontation between the old and the new permeates medieval Latin literature, [4] is the basis of the question of the *autores*, [5] and is the immediate impulse behind Isidore's monumental codification of the learning of the past into the *Origenes*. [6] It is a confrontation which seeks its ultimate resolution, albeit a bit tardily, in St. Thomas Aquinas's harmony of Christian theology and pagan philosophy. Figural interpretation is predicated on the common

---

[4] See Auerbach, pp. 28-49. Henry Osborn Taylor, *The Classical Heritage of the Middle Ages* (New York, 1958), writes with respect to art that "the Christian authors had renounced the pagan religion, they condemned its idolatry, some of them disapproved pagan literature. But one and all were educated in standards of artistic taste and principles of literary composition which were the fruit of pagan culture. ... But these classic rules were profoundly irreconcilable with the spirit and demands of the new Christian matter, as may be readily seen in Christian poetry" (p. 7). C. S. Lewis, *The Discarded Image: An Introduction to Medieval and Renaissance Literature* (Cambridge, Eng., 1964), has attempted to show how the Middle Ages may be viewed as an attempt to construct and maintain "a single, complex, harmonious mental Model of the Universe" (p. 11) on the basis of the learning of classical antiquity as it is absorbed and reshaped by Christianity.

[5] Cf. Lewis's thesis in *The Discarded Image* concerning the "overwhelming bookish or clerkly character of medieval culture. ... Every writer, if he possibly can, bases himself on an earlier writer, follows an auctour [sic] preferably a Latin one" (p. 5). Ernst Robert Curtius, *European Literature and the Latin Middle Ages,* trans. Willard R. Trask (New York, 1953), makes extensive reference to the *auctores*. See in particular "Literature and Education — 5. Curriculum Authors," pp. 48-54.

[6] Curtius believes that "the *Etymologiae* ... contains a compendium of universal literary history. This characterization may seem pretentious for Isidore's scanty chronographic notices. But when they are taken together with the related material treated in various sections of the *Etymologiae*, the result is a stock of information concerning the theory and history of literature, which the Middle Ages could find in no other writer" (p. 450). Of particular interest is the contemporary belief exemplified in Isidore's writings concerning the direct line of descent of all known literatures, a belief which in itself is based on the same principle as figural interpretation. Curtius summarizes: "The theory of the primacy of Israel in the development of culture, and of Greece as the pupil of Biblical wisdom—which, though he did not originate it, was safeguarded by his authority—represents a harmonistics which, if primitive, was nevertheless extremely influential. If the poetic genres of Antiquity stemmed from Israel, that very fact also legitimized them from the Christian standpoint" (p. 456).

medieval belief that the New Testament (the new order of the universe) was a fulfillment of the prophecies of the Old Testament and represented a continuance of the past. As Christian allegory, figural interpretation attempted to see the whole of human history as one continuous stream of events characterized at one point by the fulfillment of the prophecies through the Coming of Christ, but now directed toward the fulfillment of the new prophecy, the Second Coming of Christ and the Last Judgment. [7] Each event and each individual stood in a definable relationship to the present, the past, and the future.

If one accepts the validity of this distinction between allegory and figural interpretation, he has the means for explaining the profound differences which distinguish the *Divina commedia,* perhaps the highpoint of medieval literature and certainly the paramount example of figural interpretation in literature, from *Le Roman de la Rose,* a typical work of allegory and personification. [8] Figural interpretation in turn offers the possibility of explaining several aspects of medieval Spanish literature which have normally been classed as allegory. By the fifteenth century, the newer, humanistically inspired poets had basically lost the sense of conflict between the old and the new orders, [9] and figural interpretation weakened as a

---

[7] Nevertheless, it is precisely because the final plan of God has not been fulfilled yet that sin (from the fall of man in the old order) still exists in the world alongside the saving grace brought by the new order. St. Augustine writes in the *De civitate Dei* (which is *both* the Church ["peregrenantis in hoc saeculo civitatis Dei, hoc est ecclesiae" (15,26)] and the City of God according to the final plan) that "Ergo et nunc ecclesia regnum Christi est regnumque caelorum. Regnant itaque cum illo etiam nunc sancti eius, aliter quidem, quam tunc renabunt; nec tamen cum illo renant zizania, quamvis in ecclesia cum tritico crescant" (20,9). For the modern reader, the anachronistic" concept that "everything is resolved in the mind of God, and history is merely the working out of His Plan" is often a bit difficult to reconcile with our present view of history. However, as Auerbach points out in his *Typologische Motive in der mittelalterlichen Literatur* (Krefeld, 1953), it is such a concept which bestows validity upon figural interpretation for the medieval mind. The several periods, events, and men of history are related figurally by virtue of their role in God's plan.

[8] See Auerbach's concluding remarks concerning Dante in the article "Figura," as well as his *Dante: Poet of the Secular World.*

[9] See in passing David W. Foster, "The Misunderstanding of Dante in XVth Century Spanish Poetry," *Comparative Literature* 16 (Fall, 1964):338-47. With respect to the Renaissance, Otis Green, *Spain and the Western Tradi-*

practice, yielding to the more decorative and allegorical works of the Renaissance. [10] During the baroque period, however, it again appears as a point of departure in the *autos* and other religious literature. [11]

There is a problem involved in discussing figural interpretation in literary texts. [12] Figural interpretation was never intended to play a role in literary composition and commentary. Yet, one can point to writings in the premodern European literatures of all languages

---

tion, 4 vols. (Madison, Wis., 1963-1966), 3:190-202, "The poets feign," and 3:423-25, "Poetry and Religion," discuss some interesting examples of the accommodation of pagan mythology with the Christian concept of history and prefigurement.

[10] A rapid review of the more than hundred texts included in Léo Rouanet's collection, *Colección de autos, farsas y coloquios del siglo XVI* (Barcelona, 1901), reveals many *autos* which would be included in this study, were we concerned with the literary history of the figural motif in Spanish lyric and dramatic poetry. It is worth noting, however, that in partial defense of a study excluding the analysis of all texts making use of figural symbolism, the sixteenth-century *autos* are monotonous in their combination and re-combination of the same figural phraseology, the same anachronistic the-matics, the same generous combination of biblical personages and abstract personification, and the same "charming" intermingling of the serious (in *stilus gravis*) and the comic (*stilus humilis*). The selected (and, I hope, superior) examples studied in this monograph are exemplary of a prolific vein of sixteenth-century dramatic religious poetry, a poetry which lacks the flexible originality of the medieval texts considered.

[11] For an example in baroque religious drama, see David William Foster, "Calderón's *La torre de Babilonia* and Christian Allegory," *Criticism* 9 (Spring, 1967): 142-54.

[12] One must make a very basic distinction between the religious use of the figural tradition to explain history and the Old Testament, in which the intent is to account for all of history in terms of its prefigurement of the pres-ent and the way in which the present prefigures in turn God's final plan of the universe; and figural interpretation as a secular writer uses it in order to account for human events and behavior, and his dependence on antiquity for literary models. In the latter instances, the poet need only account for what he chooses. However, it is only natural that the secular poet depend on the Christian tradition and its interpretation of history. Chydenius discusses the problem which arose during the Middle Ages concerning the validity of using the figural interpretation on events other than those mentioned in the Bible: "The distinction of St. Thomas between the typical signification of Scripture and the allegory used in poetry, indicated that the fundamental difference between Christian typology and Greek allegory was again discov-ered after the confusion of the early Middle Ages. It remained only for it to be made clear that this difference does not exclude the possibility of typical signification being found in works of literature other than the Sacred Scriptures" (p. 44).

which evince the strong link in our culture between Christianity and the creative literature by Christians. Such a strong link has given rise to an orientation, especially in English literary criticism, known as "panallegorism." It is an orientation which would approach all medieval literature as a model of the figural concept of mankind and history or of Christian sacramental symbolism. [13] There are nevertheless many methodological arguments against imposing one critical frame of reference on a rich and diversified literary tradition. More plausible is the restriction of critical interest to those works which undeniably employ the divine plan as a structural motif. [14] Thus we take no special interest in those works whose use of the signs and symbols of sacramental/figural interpretation is more properly defined as casual, or in those works to whose coherent profane meaning we may assign an alternate divine meaning. The latter certainly respond to allegory in a limited and exegetical sense. However, the poetry which this study discusses is religious in nature, and it will be shown that it is religious in reference as well. While it may not be possible to demonstrate the use of Christian allegory in all of medieval literature, it is unquestionably present in many of the most important works of religious inspiration. In Spain, this is particularly true for the thirteenth century when the medieval Latin tradition began to exercise its greatest effect. An understanding of the role of figural interpretation in these works will contribute to the understanding of their structure in terms of the artist's own conception of the unity of human reality. [15]

---

[13] See the series of articles, "Patristic Exegesis in the Criticism of Medieval Literature," in Dorothy Bethurum, *Critical Approaches to Medieval Literature* (New York, 1960), pp. 1-82; see in particular, Charles Donahue, "Patristic Exegesis: Summation," pp. 61-82. The panallegorical approach in Spanish criticism is exemplified by Thomas Hart's papers, on which we will have the occasion to comment in the discussions which follow.

[14] An excellent application of this latter approach is John Dennis Hurrell, "The Figural Approach to Medieval Drama," *College English* 26 (1964-1965): 598-604.

[15] Hurrell makes the provocative observation that medieval drama (we may add, literature in general) is more sophisticated and less naive than we moderns are wont to admit when we impose on it artistic standards of the Renaissance or of our own day: "What this reasoning does not allow for is an understanding of a form of drama which as a form is not dependent on 'unity and economy,' not confined to being either historical or contemporary, serious or comic: a drama which we can call 'agglutinative' in its

Consider for example Thomas R. Hart's paper on the ballad "Conde Arnaldos," in which he provides an interesting discussion of the most famous of the Spanish ballads in terms of the scriptural tradition. [16] Hart discusses scriptural allegory, mentioning the process of reading for the *nucleus* of meaning beyond the *cortex,* a practice stimulated by the scriptural exegesis of the Old Testament—the cortex—for the nucleus of Christian prophecy which it contained. Usually, although not necessarily, the relationship between the cortex and the nucleus is precisely the figural interpretation of texts; the reading may, however, also yield a strictly allegorical interpretation of the Hellenistic variety. Hart attempts to show that the count is a Christ figure and that the various mysterious symbols of the poem, which have alternately bewildered and delighted readers, are tropological symbols of Christ and the Church. Hart's procedure differs from the one employed in this study in several respects, and therefore I have excluded the ballad in question from the present study. In the first place, Hart approaches the poem with a particular procedure for reading and interpreting texts. He requires us to imitate the medieval reader, with his concept of cortex-nucleus for all, or almost all, texts. The text in question is not apparently allegorical or figural in nature. Hart is not primarily interested in explaining an obvious structure, but is attempting to attribute a particular one to the work. A posteriori, the interpretation and the allegorical framework appear valid, although it is open to question and disagreement by one who would reject the necessary cortex-nucleus point of departure in the mind of the reader—or the author. This study, however, deals with figural interpretation not as a technique for the reading of texts, but as a point of departure for showing how certain patterns of association are part of a structure. Thus, in the majority of the texts analyzed, the figural frame of reference is boldly integrated in the cortex—the literal level—of the work, rather than being a

---

effect without using the term pejoratively; a drama which is like this because its authors saw their world as a place with an organic unity of time and place, body and spirit [by the same token, concrete and abstract], and had no need for, perhaps would not have understood, the theory of an artificially imposed artistic unity which has no connection with the true facts of human life" (p. 599).

[16] " 'El Conde Arnaldos' and the Medieval Scriptural Tradition," *Modern Language Notes* 72 (1957):281-85.

hidden meaning or truth for the critic to discover. Figural interpretation represented a particular range of ideas available to the poet
in the elaboration of his poem; this study attempts to show different uses of the figural structure. The question of whether the
medieval reader read all serious poetry—and perhaps even satiric
and farcical poetry as well—in terms of the scheme of Christian redemption belongs more properly to the study of the sociology of
literature in medieval culture than to the study of poetic rhetoric.
Thus, I have excluded several works which I am tempted to read
in the same way as Hart has read the "Conde Arnaldos."

Contemporary critics insist that form and content are inseparable
and unrecognizable as distinct entities as far as the work of literature
is concerned — that, in short, structure *is* meaning. This neo-
Aristotelian approach places an enormous emphasis on the work
of literature as the elaboration and realization of form. The critic
is encouraged to be aware of the subtle ways a poet organizes his
material for the greatest density and unity of meaning. There are
many areas of early poetry open to examination from the point
of view of such a critical persuasion: there is perhaps no body of
literature more sensitive to the exigencies of formalized expres-
sion, although we often tend to forget that unity in medieval
literature is not necessarily in agreement with modern concepts of
unity. In this study, I undertake to probe one aspect of medieval
poetry to demonstrate how attention to organization can reveal the
difference in procedure underlying two modes of allegory which,
from a less formalistic point of view, have usually been treated
identically.

CHAPTER I

THE CONCEPT OF FULFILLMENT AND THE
UNITY OF DIVINE HISTORY

INHERENT IN THE FIGURAL CONCEPT OF HISTORY is the role of prophecy. Fulfilled history bespeaks the way in which God has ordered
the universe so that the present is a realization of the past, while
new figures are to be understood as God's prophecy of the future
history of mankind. Christianity firmly believed in the prophecy of
the Old Testament and continues to heed the promises of the New
Testament with respect to the final Kingdom of God.

Strictly speaking, only the Old Testament presented a coherent
prophecy of Christianity. Yet, many thinkers came to respect all of
the literary and cultural manifestations of antiquity as in some way
foretelling the Coming of Christ and the salvation of mankind.
Virgil, for example, was highly respected during the Middle Ages
on the basis of his having supposedly foretold the coming of a
savior in the Fourth Eclogue. Therefore, it is justifiable to suppose
that Dante accords the Latin poet such an important role in the
Divina commedia precisely because of the Roman poet's fame in
the Middle Ages as a prophet of the New Law. [1] Although
there are scant consistent and elaborate interpretations of pre-
Christian literature and mythology in terms of the figural concept of

---

[1] Ernst Robert Curtius, *European Literature and the Latin Middle Ages,*
trans. Willard R. Trask (New York, 1953), mentions the importance of Virgil
and other pagan figures as prophets in chapter 11, "Poetry and Philosophy."
See also chapter 17, "Dante."

revelation, occasional reference may be found to works and men who in one way or another are revered for having prefigured Christ. [2]

Church scholars devoted themselves to the analysis of the Old Testament as the major text of Christian prefigurement, but the poets, more concerned with creative literature and less interested in the niceties of theology, were ingenious in utilizing pagan culture within the Christian framework. [3] Often the poets' accommodation is not particularly subtle; nor is it impressive in proving that pagan culture elaborated a prophecy of Christianity. More often than not, the allusion to or use of pre-Christian men and events represents an exercise in association whereby the poet demonstrates an interest in placing the Christian story in a new light. Nevertheless, there are occasional pieces to which the critic can point, works in which a clichéd concept of history and mankind is galvanized into a particularly original work of art. In the sections which follow, emphasis is placed not on works which reveal an ordinary utilization of Christian allegory—certainly many are passed over silently—but rather on compositions which contribute to understanding the structural realization of a vision of human destiny by an early poet.

One of the best and earliest examples of such a unified elaboration of figural structure is to be found in the *Auto de los Reyes*

---

[2] I am not here referring to those works of medieval ethics which "read" a myth or a work of pagan antiquity in terms of Christian morals and ethics. Works such as the *Ovide moralisé* (fourteenth century) represent the attempt to accommodate a particularly popular work in such a way as to exploit its popularity as a vehicle for moral doctrine. Such an accommodation usually ignored the integrity of the original text. On the other hand, figural accommodation of texts pretended to see inherent in the literal sense of the original, maintained intact, the higher meaning of revelation. It is true, however, that at times the exegetes and the poets in their endeavor to see the Christian revelation prophesied in the works of antiquity resorted to interpretations as farfetched as the moral doctrinarians.

[3] Again, one may point to Dante as a superb example of the use of pagan mythology within a Christian framework. Each of the circles of the *Inferno*—itself an adaptation of the Hades of Virgil's *Aeneid,* VI—is guarded by a beast or a figure from the pre-Christian tradition, but now put to the service of the Christian concept of hell. Hades, and the various guardians, are in their original setting prefigurements of the "true" hell of Christianity, a new truth which they fulfill and acknowledge in Dante's poem. With few exceptions, it is not until the literature of the Renaissance that we find pagan culture free from the temptation of the poet to accommodate it to the Christian framework.

Magos (ca. 1200), one of the shortest, most unique, and best-known compositions of the Middle Ages. [4] The *Auto* may be divided into three parts: the three kings' awareness of the Coming of the Messiah and their decision to seek him out (scenes 1 and 2), the communication of their discovery and decision to Herod and his reaction to their information (scenes 3 and 4), and the rabbinical confirmation of the wise men's discovery (scene 5). [5] The basic figural conflict of the *Auto* is to be found in the opposition between Christ and Herod. [6] The earthly king fears that his power will be usurped by the newcomer:

> ¿Quin uio numquas tan mal,
> Sobre rei otro tal!
> Aun non so io morto,

---

[4] This discussion of the *Auto* originally appeared in David William Foster, "Figural Interpretation and the *Auto de los Reyes Magos*," *Romanic Review* 58 (February, 1967): 3-11. My text, including erratic punctuation, is according to Ramón Menéndez Pidal, *Revista de archivos, bibliotecas y museos* 4 (1900): 453-62.

[5] I am aware of the dangers of basing a unified interpretation on a fragment. However, it is highly likely that the concluding scenes of the *Auto* would not alter the character of those which we possess. According to Ángel Valbuena Prat, *Historia de la literatura española,* 5a ed. (Barcelona, 1957): "Falta el desenlace de la pieza, aunque podemos suponer que pondría en escena la adoración ante el portal de Belén. Acaso pudiéramos pensar en la no imposibilidad de un 'villancico' primario, rudo, que correspondiese al mismo grado lírico y cantable del 'Eya, velar' de un poema de Berceo. Tal como se halla la pieza es la primera forma de lo que será el 'auto del Nacimiento' de los siglos XV y XVI" (1:67). B. W. Wardropper, "The Dramatic Texture of the 'Auto de los Reyes Magos'," *Modern Language Notes* 70 (1955): 46-50, is very much aware of the New Law and the Old Law and the problem of the relationship between the "King of Earth" and the "King of Heaven," although the possibility of figural interpretation as the basis of the relationship does not seem to occur to him. Concerning the matter of medieval dramatic unity on the basis of figural interpretation, see John Dennis Hurrell's excellent article, "The Figural Approach to Medieval Drama, *College English* 26 (1965): 598-604, in which he discusses certain aspects of medieval English drama.

[6] It is important to note the striking difference between a work such as the *Auto de los Reyes Magos,* in which the figural motif underlies certain structural characteristics, and a work such as Hernando de Yanguas's *Égloga en loor de la Natividad de nuestro Señor* or Fernando Díaz's *Farsa* (both sixteenth-century), in which figural references are present in the speech of *pastores* who stand around and talk about the fulfillment of the prophecies, without any figural motif being an issue of structure. See texts in Eugen Kohler, *Sieben spanische dramatische Eklogen* (Dresden, 1911), pp. 192-209, 317-28.

no so la terra pusto!
rei otro sobre mi?
numquas atal non ui!
El seglo ua a caga
ia non se que me faga;
por uertad no lo creo
ata que io lo ueo.

(vv. 107-16)

Herod is not aware that his rival is more than a threat to his temporal authority, but is the Savior who has come to fulfill the prophecy of a universal Messiah and leader of mankind—a Prince of Peace whose authority extends far beyond the limits of Herod's domain. As a result, Herod's cry "El seglo ua a caga" (v. 113) is charged with the irony born of his ignorance of the identity of the newborn child. Things have not gone bad and the world has not gone backward," but rather forward toward the fulfillment of God's promise. Herod is a figure of the old order of the universe who in his royalty assumes the role of a worldly king before the Coming of Christ. Christ, the fulfillment of the prophecies and the figures of the old order, supplants the old order and becomes a figure of the new order of the universe and of its prophecies of the Last Judgment of man. One of the rabbis called by Herod informs him of this fact, upbraiding the other for his ignorance of the prophecies:

(Herodes)
Pues catad,
dezid me la uertad,
si es aquel omne nacido
que esto tres rees m' an dicho.
Di, rabi, la uertad, si tu lo as sabido.

(El Rabí)
Po[r] ueras uo lo digo
que no lo [fallo] escripto.

(Otro Rabí al Primero)
Hamihala, cumo eres enartado!
por que eres rabi clamado?
Non entendes las profecias,
las que nos dixo Ieremias.

(vv. 131-41)

The three wise men fulfill an intermediary role in the *Auto*. It is they who read the book of the heavens[7] and ascertain the fulfillment of the scripture (scene 1), then decide to undertake the journey to find the Savior and to test the extent of his powers:

> (Caspar)
> Nos imos otrosi, sil podremos falar.
> Andemos tras la strela, ueremos el logar.
>
> (Melchior)
> Cumo podremos prouar si es homne mortal
> o si es rei de terra o si celestrial?
>
> (Baltasar)
> Queredes bien saber cumo lo sabremos?
> oro, mira i acenso a el ofrecremos:
> si fure rei de terra, el oro quera;
> si fure omne mortal, la mira tomara;
> si rei celestrial, estos dos dexara,
> tomara el encenso quel pertenecera.
>
> (vv. 63-72)

Although we lack the conclusion of the work, in which the Child would have been offered the three gifts, we can foresee, as the audience would have been able to foresee at this point, the three gifts being accepted in turn, thus establishing the new King's nature and affirming conclusively the new order of the universe.

A figural relationship also exists between the three wise men and the rabbis. While the three are not ministers of Christ, they speak for the Savior when they bear news of their discovery to Herod. The superiority of their knowledge and their willingness

---

[7] Wardropper, p. 47. He footnotes a reference to Curtius's chapter 16, "The Book as Symbol." As for the general signs and symbols to which I refer, I have based my assertions on a wide variety of sources, although my interpretations are obvious from the context in which they appear. I have considered it pedantic padding to quote extensively from contemporary patristic literature. (The critic often overlooks the "philological fallacy"; i.e., that, if works *A* through *Y* iterate a specific characteristic, *Z* must also conform. Such a fallacy leads to much irrelevant overreference to other works and a lack of emphasis on the originality of the work in question.) My two sources for verifying my assertions are George Furguson, *Signs and Symbols in Christian Art* (New York, 1961), and Walter B. Fulghum, Jr., *A Dictionary of Biblical Allusions in English Literature* (New York, 1965).

to accept the wonder of what they have read in the heavens would have won them the instant sympathy of the medieval audience:

> (Caspar)
> Rei, uertad te dizremos,
> que prouado lo auemos.
>
> (Melchior)
> Esto es grand ma[ra]uila.
> un strela es nacida.
>
> (Baltasar)
> Sennal face que es nacido
> i in carne humana uenido.
>
> (vv. 90-95)

These lines contrast with the contradictory reports of the rabbis. The learned men of the old order fight among themselves as to what has occurred, to the hearty disapproval of the spectators. [8] They acknowledge the truth only when it has been pointed out that the universe has altered. But they are unable to accept that truth as their own:

> (Otro Rabí al Primero)
> ... Par mi lei, nos somos erados!
> por que non somos acordados?
> por que non dezimos uertad?
>
> (Rabí Primero)
> Io non la se, par caridad.

---

[8] It seems that both the offering of gifts and the disputation of the rabbis are unique to the *Auto* and represent particular problems of interpretation owing to the fragmentary nature and imperfect quality of the manuscript. See W. Studervant, *The Misterio de los Reyes Magos: Its Position in the Development of the Medieval Legend of the Three Kings* (Baltimore, Md., 1927). Studervant's conclusions are appropriately moderate in that he finds nothing to contradict either accepted theological tradition or standard treatments of the subject (pp. 77-78). The other point of interest is the discussion of the degree of similarity to the Latin liturgical plays (pp. 46-55). Without entering into this discussion, suffice it to say that a strong connection between the Spanish and the Latin works might go far toward explaining the use of the figural interpretation, which has its immediate roots in the medieval Latin treatment of scripture and liturgical themes.

(Rabí Segundo)
Por que no la auemos usada,
ni en nostras uocas es falada.

(vv. 142-47)

Thus, despite the favorable position which they enjoy by accident in the fragment, the rabbis are overshadowed by the three wise men.

Like much other medieval literature, the *Auto* demonstrates "cultural projection." The past is seen in terms of the present, and personages from the past speak as though they were contemporary to the author or spectator. The relation of this phenomenon to figural interpretation is not difficult to understand, since it is based on the belief that all divine history has been resolved in the mind of God. A good example of cultural projection in the *Auto* occurs when Caspar says "nacido es Dios, por uer, de fembra / in achest mes de december" (vv. 15-16). Here the author puts the later established convention of Christ's December birthday into the mouth of the wise man. The same process accounts for the seeming disparity between the wise men's wholehearted acceptance of the message of the heavens and the Coming of the Messiah (vv. 1-64) and Melchior's concern over how they are to know the extent of his powers (vv. 65-72). Within the framework of the medieval spectator's absolute acceptance of the portent of the skies, the drama of recognition and establishment of the new order is worked out. The same secure recognition is present in instances where the wise men speak in language directly reminiscent of the New Testament.

Herod calls for his learned men to explain the three wise men's report on the basis of their books:

(Herodes, solo)
... Idme por mios abades
I por mis podestades,
i por mios scriuanos,
i por meos gramatgos,
i por mios retoricos;
dezir m'an la uertad, si iace in scripto,
o si lo saben elos, o si lo an sabido.

(vv. 119-26)

... I traedes ustros escriptos?

(v. 128)

(Los Sabios)
Rei, si traemos,
los meiores que nos auemos.

(Herodes)
Pus catad,
dezid me la uertad,
si es aquel omne nacido
que esto tres rees m'an dicho.
Di, rabi, la uertad, si tu lo as sabido.

(El Rabí)
Po[r] ueras uo lo digo
que no lo [fallo] escripto.

(vv. 129-37)

Subsequently, the rabbis discover their error and admit that the
event was foretold in another book (i.e., the Old Testament), of
which they are ignorant. Thus, not only are their books superseded
by the prophecies (here, of Jeremiah), but the prophet has now been
supplanted by the fulfillment of his own prophecies, to be read in
the firmament. Melchior is quick to realize that although he can
find no evidence of the star in his books ("Ual, Criador, atal facinda
/ fu nunquas alguandre falada / o en escriptura trubada?" vv. 33-
35), such an event replaces his scholarly references, and he accordingly believes after only the slightest of hesitations: "Es? non Es? /
cudo que uerdad es" (vv. 44-45). Such is the dramatic unity of the
Auto. [9] There is little relation here to allegory, and allegory has not
been considered a likely rhetorical component of the *Auto.*

Narrower in its thematic focus and more uninhibitedly anachronistic in its perspective is the anonymous thirteenth-century (?)

---

[9] An example of an extended, nonfragmentary version of the story is to
be found in the late sixteenth-century "Comedia ... de la historia y adoración
de los tres rreyes magos ...," ed. Carl Allen Tyre, "Religious Plays of 1590,"
University of Iowa Studies in Spanish 8 (1938):21-37. The two works are
almost identical in the ironies, figural conflicts, and anachronistic perspective
which they elaborate. The later *auto* concludes with the following *Canción:*

Nueba vida, nueba ley,
nuebos rrayos, nueba estrella,
nuebo Niño, nuebo Rrey,
nueba parida Donzella.

(vv. 552-55)

Catalan biblical legend, "Dels diners on fo venut Jhesuchrist." [10] The poem relates the origin of the thirty pieces of silver for which Christ was betrayed, and has a very definable figural structure. The first part of the poem concludes with the purchase with the money of a burial site for pilgrims who die in Jerusalem and a description of the crucifixion of Christ (vv. 1062-1202). Then follows a longer segment (vv. 1203-1315) in which the successful quest for the cross, nails, and crown of thorns by Constantine's mother, Elena, is related. The tone between the two segments is markedly different and the question arises as to whether two separate poems are involved. However, the editor presents them as one (supposedly with good reason), and the fact that the transition between the two parts is not easily defined leads us to attempt a unified interpretation of the composition on the basis of the established text.

The first segment dwells upon fourteen holders of the thirty fateful pieces of silver, presenting the reader with a brisk narrative of their passage from one hand to another. Although a knowledge of the "true" set of facts produces a certain amount of bemusement over the fancifulness of the legend, a closer examination reveals that the poet has relied on such an anachronistic approach to divine history for purposes of highlighting and underlining the strong link between the personages and events of the Old Law and the fulfillment of the New. For example, the money passes from lo rey Nin, who has it minted, to Abram, Josep, lo rey Pharao, Salamo, Nabugodonosor, los tres Reys d'Aurient, the Jewish temple, Judas traydor. Note that the general progression begins with several Old Law prophets, frequently interpreted by the figural exegetical tradition as Christ types—Joseph is one of the most popular, and the poet accordingly modifies the biblical tale in order to have Joseph sold by his brothers for the thirty pieces, instead of the correct number of twenty. [11] Next the poet stresses how the coins came

---

[10] Text in Joan Corominas, "The Old Catalan Rhymed Legends of the Seville Bible: A Critical Text," *Hispanic Review* 27 (1959):361-83, vv. 1062-1315.

[11] In the not quite complete fourteenth-century *Poema de José* (or *Poema de Yuçuf*), written in Spanish but using the Arabic alphabet, there is much that might be interpreted as employing the figural motif. Based on the biblical account of Joseph and his brothers (Genesis 37-50), the poem relates the selling of Joseph into captivity, his triumph and power in captivity, until

into the possession of the three wise men, who, as we have seen, play an important role in interpreting the passage from the Old to the New Law. The kings give the money to Christ. Mary buries the money when the holy family flees to Egypt, and it is found by some *pastores*. They return it to Christ, who in turn donates it to the Jewish temple. Judas is given the thirty pieces by the temple Jews, thereby establishing a direct line of descent from Christ to the anti-Christ.

The new Adam provides in the Catalan poem the means for his own betrayal, and in so having him participate actively, the anonymous poet is underlining the common figural belief that, although Jesus is betrayed, Judas's deceit is an actual historic event which correlates with and fulfills Christ's role to take upon himself the redemption of mankind through his own self-sacrifice. The thirty pieces of silver are given such an important part in the poem precisely because they represent one objective, tangible demonstration of the unified pattern of divine history. In so distorting actual events, the poet reveals not his concern for human chronology, but rather his overriding preoccupation in laying before us the progressive thread of the divine plan. By having the coins coordinate Old Law figures, the transitional and perceptive wise men, the treacherous Jewish priests, who will not accept the truth, and Christ and his antitype Judas, the poet provides his composition with a narrative cohesiveness that is not immediately apparent to the reader bewildered by the rampant narrative anachronism.

---

he is in a position to "save" his brothers from famine and to forgive them. The son of Jacob—called Israel by the Lord and one of the major pre-Christ prophets and a typical Jehovah figure—and Rachel, Joseph has often been seen as a prefigurement of Christ himself. Unfortunately, the 300-stanza Spanish poem in question generally follows the biblical account, garbling it in a few instances, without advancing any coherent vision that would enable us to say that the poet has significantly interpreted the story in such a way as to make the figural motif more than just latent by the very nature of the account. In addition, and most seriously, the poet omits one of the key incidents of the biblical account, Genesis 45:4-9, in which Joseph forgives his brothers, telling them that his captivity was preordained by the Lord to save them. Such an omission rather weakens any figural intent of the poem. But, then, perhaps the poet included it in the missing concluding fragment. In any case, as it stands, the *Poema de José* falls outside the scope of this discussion. See the edition by Ramón Menéndez Pidal (Madrid, 1952).

More than anachronistic is the second and longer segment of the poem, dealing with the recovery of the artifacts of the crucifixion. The question arises as to what the relationship is between the thirty pieces of silver, with which the poem purportedly deals, and the "crots, claus e corona," which are the center of interest from verse 1203 on. Could it be that the poet intends for us to understand a transference of figural meaning from the coins to the artifacts? The burial and recovery of the coins, their role in the betrayal, their purchasing of a burial ground on the one hand, and on the other hand the immediately subsequent account of the artifacts used to carry out Christ's passion (vv. 1195-1202) —their burial, eventual recovery, and permanent employment as symbols of Christianity— suggest a subtle attempt to force a relationship between coins and artifacts. Indeed, were we *not* to accept such a relationship, it would be impossible to assign any reasonable unity between the two conjoined segments.

Let us assume, then, that the coins, never mentioned after verse 1194, and the artifacts, presented in the following verses, are meant to enjoy a figural interrelationship. It is now possible to understand the progression of the second segment as an affirmation of the redemption of mankind by the crucifixion of Jesus, described at the conclusion of the first segment that is so significant for stressing the role of those very artifacts in the treachery of the Jews.

When Elena sets out to seek the cross, nails, and crown of thorns in Jerusalem, she is at first frustrated in her quest. However, a man offers his services and assures her that he knows where the artifacts are buried, for his grandfather had been a witness to the crucifixion. The helpful guide is a Jew named Judas, and his promise is accordingly made good. The poet, then, posits a new Judas. He is a man who, rather than betraying Christ (as had the apostle Judas in order to fulfill the design), functions in an analogous but positive role. In the latter case, God's design is fulfilled further in the "revelation by recovery" to man of the symbols of his redemption by Christ. It is thus no surprise to find that the work ends with a description of the glorification of these signs:

> Ara vos he dita ver[i]tat
> dels tres claus on [Jesús] fo claufcat,
> [e] de la vera [sancta] creu examens,
> de la corona certamens,

que sent' Elena o tramès
a Constantí [emperador], sí com dit és,
que son fiyl era, per ver[i]tat;
[e] per sant tresor li·u a donat.
[E] Constantí ·n [son] coil, devotament,
meté dins Roma, certament,
la vera [sancta] crots e la corona,
e·u donà [per tresor] (a) l[a sancta]'
      esgleya de Roma.
Dels claus féu so qu' avets ausit:
[e] enaxí es per cert escrit.

                              (vv. 1301-15)

Only if we accept the hypothesis that the thirty pieces of silver and
the artifacts are figurally related can we understand the poet's
shift in emphasis from the coins—the announced theme of the
narration—to the artifacts with which he concludes his work.

The figural equation is obvious: through Judas, the fateful thirty
pieces of silver effect Christ's betrayal and passion; through the new
Judas, the recovered artifacts effect the glorious announcement to
man of his redemption. In order to stress this clear figural equation,
the poet has the new Judas converted to Christianity—redeemed
from his sins through the powerful and efficacious influence of the
recovered artifacts:

Lo jueu Judes qu' aysò mostret
babtisme pres e no·u tardet,
Cirianus se féu nomnar;
e lo diable va<·l> cridar
la sus en l' àer e va dir:
—Sàpies que jo·t faré morir
a mala mort, cant a<s> mostrat
lo fust on Déu fo cluaficat.—
Ciria respòs: —No é paor,
que Jhesuchrist creu e aor.—
Morí lo bisbe d'aquel loc
e Cirià fo bisb' en son loc;
[aprés] por Déu pres mort e passió
e venc a vera salvació.

                              (vv. 1269-82)

In this way, the poem pushes even further its figural motifs. By
incorporating the conversion of the new Judas, not only does the

Judas figure merge with the redeemed Adam figure, but his conversion results from his participation in the recovery of the artifacts. Man's redemption—his "vera salvació"—is symbolized by the artifacts typically related to the thirty pieces of silver which, in the hands of the Judas figure of the Old Law (Judas is paid off by the Jews of the temple), represent man's betrayal of Christ as well as Christ's acceptance of the responsibility of sacrificing himself. Superficially, the Catalan rhymed "biblical" legend is choatic and haphazard. Nevertheless, as has been demonstrated, a very well planned figural unity underlies its structure.

The sacrifice of the mass constitutes the prominent, central ritual of Christianity as well as a mark in the passage from the Old to the New Law. A reenactment of the Last Supper, the mass focuses on the person of Christ as the fulfillment of the promise of salvation for mankind. In both the elevation of the Host and chalice, where the words of Christ are recited, and in the minor elevation ("Per ipsum, et in ipso, et cum ipso, est tibi Deo omnis honor et gloria"), the priest reminds the communicants of the role of Christ as the culmination of a prophecy.

One of the most singular characteristics of the Roman rite of the mass is the commingling of prayers and ritual formulas from both the Old and the New Testament traditions. Indeed, until the recent changes in the liturgy, the mass had begun with a recitation of Psalm 42, "Introibo ad altare Dei." The presence of elements of the Old Testament worship in the structure of the mass itself is an everyday reminder to the faithful of the intimate relationship in Christian doctrine and practice between the Old and the New Laws.

More significant from a historical point of view, and from the particular point of view of a history of the Judeo-Christian concept of the figural tradition of historiography, is the development of the mass as a fulfillment and a rendering in terms of the New Law of the Jewish sacrificial rites. In terms of a strictly theological—and figural—interpretation of the function of the mass, one must bear in mind its history as the commemoration of the Last Supper, which was intended to imitate or render in Christ's own terms a Jewish celebration. The passion is understood to derive its meaning and import from its concurrence with the Jewish Passover. The mass refers to Christ as the *Agnus Dei,* the Lamb of God, the Lamb of the New Law whose selfmade sacrifice fulfills the prophecy supposedly inherent in the Jewish Passover rites, while thereby also invalidating any further meaning, *post Passionem Christi,* of those rites. Thus—although this is not made as obvious to latter-day Catholics as it was to the apostles and to the early church fathers— the mass is purportedly an extension of ancient sacrificial rites, with the significant difference in the role of Christ as the voluntary sacrifice, the fulfillment of the prophecies, and the culmination of the eternal hope of mankind for redemption.

Needless to say, the mass, with its rich heritage of prayers, doxologies, extracts from the scripture of both Laws, and other formulas of ritual worship, probably ranked second only to the lives of Christ and the saints as a source of literary material in the Middle Ages. [12] Not only do we find many glosses of a serious nature, but the waning of the Middle Ages (the fourteenth and fifteenth centuries) saw the practice of parodying the mass in the poetry descendent from the courtly love tradition in the poetic genre of the "misas de amor." [13]

One of the most accomplished figural treatments of the mass is Gonzalo de Berceo's *Sacrificio de la Misa,* [14] a unified discussion

---

[12] It is important to remember that the mass attained its present form only gradually over a period of several centuries, with many rival liturgies competing for prominence and universal acceptance. At times the ensuing controversies were decidedly heated, and the writer had much material from which to choose. It is, however, safe to say that all of the liturgies attempted to keep in focus the role of the mass as a reenactment, specifically of the Last Supper, and generally of the Passion of Christ as a fulfillment of the prophecy of the Jewish Passover. The Council of Trent, 1545-1563, established the Roman rite then in practice as the "official" rite. Until the recent ecumenical changes, it is this rite which has defined the mass to western Catholics.

[13] For a discussion of the *Misa de amor,* see María Rosa Lida, "El romance del misa de amor," *Revista de filología hispánica* 3 (1941); 24-42.

[14] My text is that of the edition by Antonio G. Solalinde (Madrid, 1913). However, since his edition is paleographic, I have modified the transcription of the verses as appropriate to a critical edition. For the sources of Berceo's poem, see H. L. Schug, *Latin Sources of Berceo's "Sacrificio de la Misa"* (Nashville, Tenn., 1936). T. C. Goode, *Gonzalo de Berceo. El sacrificio de la Misa. A Study of Its Symbolism and Its Sources* (Washington, D. C., 1933), is, to my knowledge, the only discussion of Berceo or of any medieval Spanish poet to acknowledge the role of biblical allegory in creative literature. Sister Goode's approach is through the application of the fourfold exegesis of scripture, and thus, her remarks are oriented toward indicating Berceo's use of one or another of the four techniques, rather than toward an analysis of his concept of the figural interpretation of the mass. However, she is

of the mass as the fulfillment of prophecy. However, because he is dealing with what is already virtually a written document, the "text" of the mass—Berceo deals basically only with the canon of the unchanging proper of the mass—his poem is more properly a gloss, where his Marian and hagiographic literature is essentially narrative in nature. Nevertheless, Berceo does not confine himself to a summary of the mass, but proceeds to interpret and to explicate central facets. It is possible for one to argue that because of its factual nature, this work should be excluded from a discussion of creative poetry. Yet, such a position overlooks the impracticability of a sharp line of demarcation in medieval literature between the two types of texts. Because Berceo is a poet indulging in a variety of original and interesting perspectives, I have included his work in my discussion.

After a brief introductory exordium, the poet clarifies his intention to discuss the mass within the context of its relationship to the Old Testament:

> Del Testamento Uieio quiero luego fablar,
> como sacrificauan y sobre qual altar,
> desent tornar al Nueuo por enciero andar,
> acordar los en uno, fazer los saludar.
>
> (s. 2)

Then, with the words "Qvando corrie la ley de Moysen ganada [i.e., the Law of the Old Testament]" (s. 3a), Berceo begins an analysis of the implements and practices of the Jewish sacrificial rites. It is interesting to note that Berceo is respectful of the older rite and speaks of the "sancto altar" (s. 6d). Berceo's detailed analysis is significant in its length (ss. 6-17), in its acknowledgment

---

quick to emphasize Berceo's central concern: "He is struck with the harmony that exists between the two: between the *Old Law* with its Temple and its appurtenances, its priesthood and its sacrifices and the *New Law* with its Church, its sacrifice perpetually renewed on the altar, and its priesthood, representative of the eternal priesthood of Him who with His sacrifice upon the cross entered once into heaven, bearing with Him the Blood of our redemption and the fuming censer of an infinite love" (pp. 30-31). Sister Goodes' study is valuable for its detailed analysis of the poet's symbolism and provides an excellent introduction to the *Sacrificio*. My own analysis attempts to go beyond her minute examination of backgrounds and symbolism to consider the structural and artistic implications of the poet's interest in the figural meaning of the mass.

of the divine provenience of the ritual and its implements, [15] and in the prominence given the elements of worship of the Old Law in the opening section of a work purporting to deal with the Christian mass. However, the reader must answer for himself any question concerning the elements of worship described. [16] Berceo relies on his audience to understand the typological import of the Jewish sacrifice. The poet simply reminds us that:

> Todas estas offendas las auei e ganados,
> traen significança de oscuros mandados;
> todos en Iesu Cristo hi fueron acabados,
> que offrecio su carne por los nuestros peccados

> (s. 18)

After outlining the prefigurement of Christ symbolized by the "cabron," the "corderuelo," and the "palomba" (ss. 19-22), Berceo reiterates his point:

> Todos los sacrificios, los de la ley primera,
> todos significan la hostia uerdadera;
> esta fue Iesu Cristo que abrio la carrera
> porque tornar podamos ala sied cabdalera.

> (s. 22)

In affirming the role of Christ in restoring mankind to grace, Berceo reveals how his preoccupation with the mass up to this point has been allegorical. That is to say, the discussion dwells on the present, the New Law, as fulfillment and resolution of a prior order,

---

[15] At one point he describes part of the inner sanctuary:

> Reliquiario era esta archa nomnada,
> de muy sanctas reliquias era muy bien poblada;
> hi estauan las tablas en que la ley fu dada,
> la uerga de Aaron, cosa muy sennalada.
> Ena [sic, i. e., una] olla de oro, non de tierra labrada,
> plena de sancta manna del cielo embiada,
> la que alos iudios daua Dios por ceuada,
> en esta sancta archa estaua condensada.

> (ss. 14-15)

[16] Sister Goode also points this out, and proceeds to inform the modern reader of the accepted figural or Christian interpretation of each one of the elements Berceo presents. See pp. 32ff. of her study.

the Old Law. As such, the meaning assigned to the mass at this point is limited by an interpretation based on a rite linked with the fall of man. Indeed, from one point of view the mass is retrospective in its commemoration of mankind's renewed possibility of salvation, a redemption only implied figurally in the Jewish service. Thus the poet emphasizes that:

> El nuestro sacerdot quando la missa canta
> e faze sacrificio sobre mesa sancta,
> todo esto remiembra la hostia que quebranta,
> todo alli se cumpre e alli se callanta.
>
> (s. 23)

Furthermore, mankind must bear in mind that Christ's passion and sacrifice represent a complete fulfillment of the Old Law, which thus ceases to have meaning and pertinence. Referring first to a few of the standard prefigurements of Christ, the text makes clear the resolution of the Old Law:

> Sj quier los sacrificios, sequier las prophecias,
> lo que Daniel dixo, elo que Iheremias,
> e lo que Abacuc, e loque Ysayas,
> todo se encierra enla cruz de Messias.
> Qvando uino Messias todo fue aquedado:
> callaron las prophetas, el uelo fue redrado,
> folgaron los cabrones y el otro ganado;
> el puso fin atodo lo que era passado.
>
> (ss. 24-25)
>
> De que sofrio don Cristo la passion prophetada
> cumprio los sacrificios, los dela ley passada;
> leuanto la ley nueua, la uieia callantada,
> la uieia so la nueua iaze encortinada.
>
> (s. 28)

These stanzas summarize the relationship between the sacrifices of the two Laws and lead into a discussion of the higher figural meaning of the mass. The sacrifice of the mass bespeaks not only a relationship between the past and the present but also a more significant relationship between the present and the future, between the church militant and the church triumphant. The eschatological meaning of the mass immediately engages the poet's attention. He is no longer concerned solely with the relationship between the priest

of the Old Law and the priest of the New, but more with that relationship which exists between the latter and Christ. The details of
the mass described at this point derive from the following premise:

> Qvando el sancto preste assoma reuestido,
> que exe del sagrario, de logar escondido,
> a don Cristo significa que non fue entido,
> sinon nolo ouiera el traydor uendido.
>
> (s. 32)

The discussion of the role of bread and wine in the mass offers
an excellent example of how the Spaniard understands the relationship, evident in the sacrifice of the mass, between the past, the
present, and the promises of the future:

> El uino significa aDios nuestro senor,
> la agua significa al pueblo pecador;
> como estas dos cosas tornan en un sabor
> assi torna el ome con Dios en un amor.
> Qui non quier volver el agua con el vino,
> parte de Dios al omne, finca pobre mesquino;
> faze muy grant peccado pesar el rey diuino,
> qui por nos peccadores en la gloriosa uino.
> De mas, quando estaua enla cruz desbraçado,
> sangne ixio e agua del so diestro costado,
> qui partir los quisiesse farie desaguisado
> e non ferie don Cristo de tal fecho pagado.
> Abrahan, nuestro auuelo de ondrada memoria,
> quando dela fazienda tornaua con uictoria,
> offrecie Melchissedech, como diz la historia,
> pan e uino, e plogol mucho al rey de gloria.
> Offrecer pan e vino en el sancto altar,
> offrenda es autentica non podrie meiorar;
> quando con sus discipulos Cristo quiso cenar,
> con pan e uino solo los quiso comulgar.
>
> (ss. 61-65)

The presentation of the mass is more than a simple gloss on the
vestments, furniture, and gestures of the Christian sacrifice. The
analysis gains in significance and density from the very manner in
which Berceo is able to demonstrate how the history of man, Adam
the Everyman, is summarized and portrayed through the most basic
and common ritual of Christianity. The *Sacrificio de la Misa,* in its

attention to the figural structure of the mass, dwells at length upon the fall, the redemption, and the promise of salvation of man in a way that goes beyond less exegetical descriptions to engage the reader's perception of the panoramic sweep of human experience as it is understood by the Judeo-Christian concept of history, men, and events.

At this point Berceo is concerned less with interpreting the mass as a whole than with analyzing segments of the Christian ritual in terms of both their fulfillment of the Old Law and their eschatological meaning to sinful man. The poet's discussion is divided into twelve chapters, as though he were describing a text. Each chapter considers some aspect or group of aspects of the mass within the already established figural framework.

One of the most significant sections of the work concerns the figural significance of the paschal lamb (ss. 145-62). The typological symbolism of the lamb is first secured:

> Se Dios me aiudase la uoluntad complir,
> del cordero pascual uos querria dezir;
> non es de oblidar nin es de encobrir
> ca trae la figura del otro por uenir.
>
> (s. 145)

Berceo then traces the history of the paschal sacrifice in the Jewish law, dwelling on the importance of the blood of the lamb as a means of salvation. There is a careful adherence to the doctrine of the limited efficacy of the symbolic figures of the Jewish Law, along with an assurance that in their temporal effects they bespoke the eternal spiritual blessings of the prefigured Christian rite. Our immediate point of interest is first the sacrifice of Christ as fulfillment and then his eternal sacrifice as perpetuated by implication (s. 152d) in the daily sacrifice of the mass:

> Sangne saluo aessos de muerte temporal,
> nos por sangne cobramos la uida spirital;
> por sangne de cordero fino todo el mal,
> vale nos oy en dia mucho essa sennal.
>
> Iesu fue est cordero, bien parece por uista,
> mostrolo con su dedo Iohan el Baptista
> [the last Old Law prefigurement of Christ];
> la su sangne preciosa fizo esta conquista
> Algo entendio desto el rey citarista.

El cordero secundo fue de meyor oveja
mucho de meyor carne e de meyor pelleya,
ambos ouieron sangne de un color bermeia,
mas non fue la uirtut ni egual ni pareia.

La carne del primero fue en fuego assada,
La carne del segundo en la cruz maritiriada.
Por la primera sangne fue Egipto domada,
al enfierno la otra diol mala pezcoçada. [17]

La virtud dela sangne, la que postremea,
essa la fizo sancta ala sangne primera,
esta era sennora, essa otra portera,
essa fue el rostroio, esta fue la ciuera.

Semeiar mie sennores si atodos uos plaz,
al antiguo cordero fincasse en paz,
tornemos al nueuo todo nuestro solaz,
ca todo el prouecho anos en el nos iaz.

(ss. 152-57)

Thus, the major tenets of the figural doctrine are summarized in conjunction with the presentation of the paschal lamb: the ritual of the Old Law with its limited powers of solace to mankind, understood by a few prophets as the prefigurement of a more efficacious and saving grace yet to come; the fulfillment of the prefigurement through the passion and sacrifice, a fulfillment which offered to mankind a "sennal" which is of continuing validity as the quest for redemption; and, finally, the resolution and replacement of the figures of the Old Law by the figures of the New Christian Law, with their infinitely greater portent for mankind's salvation. [18] Again,

---

[17] Berceo establishes an interesting parallel here between Egypt as the "infierno" of the Jews overcome by the efficacy of the Jewish paschal lamb, and the *enfierno* of Lucifer's sin which is threatened by Christ's passion. One will recall that in the *Vida de Santa María Egipcíaca,* Egypt may be understood as a symbolic figure of the sins of Mary. Her sinful life is presented within the framework of her "voyage" to Egypt. When she is saved through Christianity, it is as a direct result of her flight from Egypt, her crossing of the River Jordan, and her trek in the desert.

[18] It is interesting to note the distinction which Berceo makes between the Jews, with their rites prefiguring Christianity, and the pagans, with their false and useless idols:

Aquelo que trascambia los brazos el abbat,
quando faz el enclin ante la maiestad,
buena es de saber esta tal puridad
si es significança o es nesciedad.

(s. 213)

we see in the interplay of the poet's referents a concern with the figural symbolism which enables him to frame historically and dynamically the Christian messianic prophecy to which he is so firmly committed.

The poet relates the integration of the paschal sacrifice with the mass and continues his gloss on the latter, emphasizing that the mass is not only a fulfillment of the Jewish sacrificial rite but also a commemoration and reenactment of the Last Supper, a figurative preview of Christ's sacrifice on the cross. Thus the poet does not fail to underscore the central role played by the mass in keeping before us the message of Christ's passion within the framework of a history of mankind's struggle for salvation and his awareness of the Christian promise of redemption in the Kingdom to come. [19]

One of Berceo's most unique interpretations concerns the Paternoster, the precommunion prayer containing the words which conclude the preceding paragraph. Referring to the importance of

---

Los iudios significan la mano mas derecha,
ca essos mantuuieron la ley sines retrecha;
essos dauan aDios sacrificos e pecha;
la tierra de Egipto por ellos fue maltrecha.
     A essos dezia fijos el nuestro Saluador,
aquessa grey buscaua como leal pastor,
elli le fizo gracia mercet e grant honor,
ella torno las coces e fizo lo peor.
     Por la siniestra mano, que es mal enbargada,
la gent de paganismo nos es significada,
ca andaua errada essa loca mesnada,
adorando los ydolos ela cosa laurada.

(ss. 215-17)

However, the poet in stanzas 218-22 remarks how the pagans were quick to follow Christ, while the Jews remained faithful to the Old Law, and thus "Los que eran por fiios dela diestra contados, / trastornosse la rueda tornaron en annados" (ss. 221a-b).

[19] Cf. stanzas 236-37:

Los sacerdotes nuestros sieruos delos altares
quando rezan el canon entre los paladares,
emientan alos sanctos por ent en dos logares,
los unos delanteros, los otros espaldares.
     Los que trayen delante demuestran los primeros,
los que traye acuestas los otros postremeros;
los uieios delos nueuos fueron bien derecheros
en fechos e en dichos iustos y uerdaderos.

the prayer, the poet emphasizes its allegorical importance when he iterates the belief that there is a higher meaning to be found beyond the surface of a work:

> El sancto "pater noster" oracion es diuina,
> de uiuos ede muertos es sancta medicina,
> non deuemos nos ende passar nos tan ayna,
> ca iace so este grano provechosa farina.

(s. 250)

Berceo then states what he believes to be the concealed importance of this prayer:

> Díxoli a Jhesucristo la su buena mesnada,
> Sant Pedro e los otros, companna esmerada:
> "sennor e padre sancto que non yerras en nada,
> "dinos como oremos oracion sennalada."
> El sennor glorioso, maestro acabado,
> vido que dician seso e tovogelo a grado,
> mostrolis el "pater noster", sermón abreviado,
> de la su sancta boca compuesto e dictado.
> Todas las oraciones menudas e granadas,
> las griegas e latinas, aqui son encerradas,
> las palabras son pocas, mas de seso cargadas,
> sabio fue el maestro que las ovo dictadas.

(ss. 252-54)

Berceo expresses here a concept unique to Spanish thirteenth-century literature, although common in the medieval Latin literary tradition: that Christian sacred literature—the liturgy, the Bible, and creative inspirational poetry as well—inherited and infused with the ultimate truth of the New Law the pre-Christian classical tradition, a tradition viewed in turn as the progressive development of Greek and Latin culture out of a dependency on the Hebrew biblical literature of the Old Law. The classical literary tradition, via its supposed Jewish backgrounds, becomes a prefiguration of the Christian tradition, and the sacred writings of Christianity fulfill, "encerrar," the secular poetry which has gone before. Thus, the Middle Ages developed the belief in the Christian prophecy inherent in certain classical texts, and the *Divina commedia* gave prominence to Virgil and other poets of antiquity as prefigurements of Dante, who considered himself the Christian poet par excellence. Concerning this "Christian accommodation" of the literary tradition of antiquity, Curtius writes: [20]

While Jerome and Isidore systematically teach the correspondence between Biblical and profane literature, and at most the chronological priority of the former, Cassiodorus carefully explores the dependence of profane upon sacred learning. The former is nothing but a development of what is contained in principle in the latter. This concept, then, substitutes a monism at once speculative and historical, for the harmonistics which, developing from the fourth century from the confluence of pagan and Christian culture, was able to effect a compromise between the dualism of the two forces but not to end it. This monistic concept is evinced in rhetorical analysis. And the result of it is a reversal of the usual literary evaluation. Now the Bible no longer needs to be justified before profane literature by a demonstration that the former too employs the recognized figures of speech—no, the figures stem from the Bible, and the Bible alone gives them their "dignity" (p. 448).

The theory of the primacy of Israel in the development of culture, and of Greece as the pupil of Biblical wisdom—which, though Isidore in the *Etymologiae* did not originate it, was safeguarded by his authority—represents a harmonistics which, if primitive, was nevertheless extremely influential. If the poetic genres of Antiquity stemmed from Israel, that very fact also legitimized them from the Christian standpoint (p. 456).

Although it is probable that Berceo was not extensively familiar with medieval Latin poetics, there is little doubt that, by one way or another, he had heard of harmonistic theories, particularly in the form in which they were propagated by Isidore, himself a Spaniard, in his widely read *Etymologiae*. Aside from any consideration of sources and influences. Berceo's lines reveal an awareness of the concept of the Christian fulfillment of classical literature. The poet refers to Christ as a "maestro" and characterizes his teaching in the Paternoster as the product of "dictar," the general term in medieval poetics for the literary act, both sacred and profane. Thus, Berceo attaches a singular importance to this most common Christian prayer, seeing it as a *Summa* of the wisdom of Christ, a wisdom inherent in one prayer which fulfills for his audience the vast teachings of the tradition of the Romans and the Greeks.

The poet further analyzes the seven requests made in the prayer, undertaking to lay bare the "provechosa farina so este grano." At

---

[20] Ernst Robert Curtius, Excursus VI "Early Christian and Medieval Literary Studies," pp. 446-67.

one point he indicates the way in which the first three petitions of the prayer [21] reveal man's expectations from God's Law:

> Estas tres peticiones que avemos leidas,
> en esti nuestro mundo nunca seran complidas
> mas seran en el otro todas bien avenidas,
> do nuevas de discordias nunca fueron oidas,
>
> (s. 258)

Berceo concludes his analysis of the Paternoster and the mass and begs his readers to offer "pater nostres" for his own and their salvation.

Two salient characteristics emerge from the preceding discussion of the *Sacrificio de la Misa*. In the first place, it is the least "artistic" of Berceo's compositions in the sense that, although we are able to discover and to analyze a sustaining figural motif, it is impossible to point to the involvement of that motif in a consistent and closely developed poetic pattern. Or, from another point of view, the poet's approach to his work as a "glosa" of the mass inhibits his organization of the subject into anything more than a loose commentary. True, we may refer to the opening stanzas where Berceo sketches the background of the mass as the fulfillment of the sacrifice of the Old Law. We might also emphasize the extensive development given the concept of the paschal lamb and the uniqueness of the point of departure for the discussion of the Paternoster. Yet, in all these instances, the poet is not interested in going beyond a commentary, and his work is dominated by a point-by-point description which takes as its model not the poetic principle of an originally conceived work of literature, but the well-established structure of the Roman rite of the mass.

Nevertheless, one must acknowledge that another dominant characteristic of the *Sacrificio de la Misa* is the poet's personal interpretation of the symbolism of the mass. Although this may not contribute toward the conception and elaboration of the poem as a unified whole, it does bestow upon it the singularity of the work of a man who is on other occasions capable of more coherent poetry. The important point is that it would be a mistake to see the *Sacrificio* as

---

[21] "Our Father who art in heaven, *hallowed be thy name, thy kingdom come, thy will be done,* on earth as it is in heaven."

merely didactic and uncreative. There is little doubt that, while Berceo may have been inspired by orthodox teachings, his approach is that of a poet. Thus, the critic's interest, properly speaking, is less in the canonical verisimilitude of Berceo's symbolism than in his interpretation of the mass as figural liturgy. As we shall see in the case of the Marian literature produced by Berceo and by other thirteenth-century Spanish poets, we are in the presence of often comically fanciful interpretations of persons and events—interpretations which have little consonance with strict Christian theology. But to be understood in their proper perspective, the production of these poets must be seen as essentially literary in provenience— theologically inspired, but decidedly the work of men who put poetic intuition before commitment to theological teaching. Such a critical tolerance does not intend to conceal the very real didactic nature of these works. Instead, it attempts to underline what one feels to be their true value and function: to communicate the Christian message poetically to an audience which was singularly and inextricably involved with the pageant and with the promise of Christianity. It is only if we understand this characteristic of the literature discussed in this study that we are able to appreciate the ways in which the poet was able to take a basic concept of the Christian tradition, the figural interpretation of human and divine history, and to shape it, to reinterpret it, and to endow it with his own personal meaning and symbolism toward the elaboration of a poetic vision of the hope and trust that man placed in his religious beliefs.

> "... Sacastes a Castiella de grand cautividat,
> fiziestes grand merçed a toda cristiandat:
> mucho pesar a moros, esto es la verdat,
> tod esto vos gradesca el Rey de Magestat."
> Todos e ella con ellos con grand gozo lloravan;
> tenien que eran muertos e que resuçitavan;
> al Rey de los çielos bendezian e laudavan,
> el llanto que fazian en grand gozo tornavan.
> (ss. 691-92)[22]

---

[22] *Poema de Fernán González,* in Ramón Menéndez Pidal, *Reliquias de la poesía épica española* (Madrid, 1951), pp. 34-156. Pidal's transcription is represented, except that I have not used the italics representing his emendations of the text.

The only known example of the "clerical" or "scholarly" epic, the thirteenth-century *Poema de Fernán González,* composed in the *cuaderna vía* tradition of the *mester de clerecía,* has only recently begun to attract critical and interpretive attention. As Américo Castro has pointed out,[23] one of the most singular characteristics of the *Poema* is its political nature, the almost mythologized nature of Castile's role in Spanish history, and the exalted place assigned Fernán González in the reconquest of the Peninsula, a reconquest which for perhaps the first time in Spanish literature is set within the framework of a holy war.[24] As a result, the relationship between myth, *leyenda,* and historical fact has been the most researched aspect of the work.[25] Nevertheless, the papers to date have not dealt with the organic unity of the *Poema* which is based upon a particular conception of Spanish history and the role of Fernán González, its champion.[26]

In the *Poema de Fernán González,* the use of the basic patterns, motifs, and symbols of the typological vision give coherence to what at first seems an absurd and exaggerated patriotic concept of Castile's struggle for survival against both Moors and assorted other agressive non-Castilians.

---

[23] Américo Castro, *The Structure of Spanish History* (Princeton, N. J., 1954), p. 163.

[24] It is worth exploring in detail the "transcendent" framework of the thirteenth-century *Poema,* a framework stressing religious and politico-national values, and the more immediate perspective of the better-known twelfth-century *Poema de Mio Cid,* which emphasizes the honor and fulfillment—the *caballerosidad*—of the individual with little reference to anything beyond social values. In this respect, the *Poema de Fernán González* is probably the much closer of the two to the *Chanson de Roland,* a poem which has been discussed as exemplifying a religious conception of history. See Karl Heisig, "Die geschichtsmetaphysik des Rolandsliedes und ihre Vorgeschite," *Zeitschrift für romanische Philologie* 55 (1935): 1-87.

[25] See J. Pérez de Urbel, "Historia y leyenda en el 'Poema de Fernán González,'" *Escorial* 14 (1944); 319-52; J. P. Keller, "El misterioso origen de Fernán González," *Nueva revista de filología hispánica* 10 (1956): 41-44; A. D. Deyermond, "Una nota sobre el *Poema de Fernán González,*" *Hispanófila* 8 (1960): 35-38; T. G. Armistead, "La perspectiva histórica del 'Poema de Fernán González,'" *Papeles de Son Armadans* 21 (1961): 9-18.

[26] See, however, J. P. Keller's important and suggestive essay, "The Structure of the *Poema de Fernán González,*" *Hispanic Review* 25 (1957): 235-46. "Structure" is, unfortunately, used here in a very loose sense. Several important observations are, nevertheless, discussed in detail, primarily the importance of the number three, to which we return below.

Our poet's conception is, as T. G. Armistead has observed, remarkably anachronistic:

"el monje atribuye a los héroes del pasado unas hazañas paralelas a las victorias del momento actual. Esto explica que las tempranas victorias de Fernán González se describan en términos propios de las etapas avanzadas de la Reconquista, llenas de viva e inmediata realidad para el poeta. Tal es el motivo de que el monje viera en su héroe no sólo el comienzo, sino también la culminación del largo proceso de la Reconquista. ... Los hechos del pasado fueron así vistos como calco del presente, como trasunto de lo actual. El poeta proyectó la Reconquista hacia el pasado y la convirtió en un proceso milenariamente reiterado. Para el monje de Arlanza, castellano del siglo XIII, carecía de realidad una España en que no existiera la oposición agónica y ya cinco veces secular de cristianos y moros. [27]

From the very outset Castile, the heartland of the Spanish Peninsula, is cast as the "chosen land of the chosen people." The poet immediately establishes the central conflict between the Moors, who are portrayed not as an opposing religious force, but as anti-Christians, and the Spaniards, who are identified as the bearers of Christ's law:

> Esto fizo Mafomat, el de la mala creençia,
> ... ...
> ca preico por su boca mucha mala sentençia.
> Desque ovo Mafomat a todos predicados,
> avian essas gentes los cueres demudados,
> ... ...
> de la muerte de Cristo seian olvidados.
> Desque los españones a Cristo conosçieron,
> desque en la su ley bautismo resçibieron,
> nunca en otra ley tornar se non quisieron,
> mas por guarda d'aquesto muchos males sufrieron.
> Esta ley de los santos que oyeron preicada,
> por ella la su sangre ovieron derramada,
> apostoles e martires, esta santa mesnada,
> fueron por la verdat metidos a espada.
> Fueron las santas virgines en est afirmamiento:
> de varon non quisieron ningun ayuntamiento,
> de los viçios del mundo non ovieron taliento,
> vençieron por aquesto al bestion mascariento.

---

[27] Armistead, "Poema de Fernán González," pp. 13-14.

Las primeras profetas esto profetizaron,
los santos confessores esta ley predicaron,
ca en los otros dioses verdat nunca fallaron,
san Juan lo afirmo quando l' descabeçaron.
Muchos reyes e condes e muchas potestades,
papas e arçobispos, obispos e abades,
por esta ley murieron, esto bien lo creades,
por end han en los çielos todas sus heredades.

(ss. 7-13)

Underpinning this evaluation of the conflict between the hosts of Christ and the hosts of the anti-Christ is the poet's unique appraisal of the Castilians' holy origin. Accommodating the Jewish theme of divine election, the poet traces Castile's supremacy back to the arrival of the Goths, still a non-Christian tribe purportedly sent by Christ to the Peninsula out of the East:

Venieron estos godos de partes d' oriente,
Cristo los enbio, est pueblo descreyente;
del linax de Magog vino aquesta yente,
conquirieron el mundo, esto sin fallimiente.
Non fueron estos godos de comienço cristianos,
nin de judios d' Egito, nin de ley de paganos;
antes fueron gentiles unos pueblos loçanos,
eran por en batalla pueblos muy venturados.

(ss. 15-16)

The stanzas which follow detail the Goths' dominion of the Roman territories and their entrenchment in the Peninsula by divine aid ("Cristus los quiso guiar," s. 19d). Inspired by the Holy Spirit —"Fueron de Sancti Spiritus los godos espirados" (s. 20a)—the Goths renounce paganism and accept Christianity:

Rescibieron los godos el agua a bautismo,
fueron luz e estrella de todo el cristianismo,
alçaron cristiandat, baxaron paganismo:
el cond Ferran Gonçalez fizo aquesto mismo.
... ...
que fue muy leal miente de sus omnes servido;
fueron de tod el mundo pueblo muy escojido,
quanto el mundo durare non cadran en olvido.

(ss. 23-24)

Note that this Ferran Gonçalez is not the hero of the poem, but a historical forerunner. The mention of him at this juncture, besides any historical reasons, is probably to imply a relationship between Ferran Gonçalez, the first Christian leader, and Fernán González of the *Poema,* the champion and savior of Castilian Christianity for the descendents of the ancestral Gothic leaders. Although the relationship is not a description which is validated by the subsequent stanzas which detail the lineage of the Gothic kings, culminating in the sinful betrayal of Rodrigo, "el último rey godo," the motifs of sin, fall, and betrayal of Christianity from within—all introduced in this segment of the *Poema*—constitute a fundamental point of departure for the poem. The "Captivity of Castile / Christianity," referred to repeatedly in the work (see the prefatory quotation where the hero is credited finally with the release from captivity), is a misfortune which comes from within, and the Moorish anti-Christs only represent the Lord's wrathful visitation on his sinful subjects. A failure to grasp the interplay between sinful Christians and the satanic legions of the Moors, however, is to misunderstand why the central segment of the poem (ss. 191-585, out of 768 surviving stanzas), deals cyclically with, first, an encounter with the Moors, then with hostile Christian Navarrese, and then again with the Moors (parts 2-4 in Menéndez Pidal's segmentation).

In dealing with the fall of Spain and the Moorish invasion, the poet elaborates a framework of prophecy and figural interrelationships, all bound up with the historical myth of the deceit, betrayal of sin from within:

> Ovieron a fer todo lo que el rey mandava,
> quien las armas tenia luego las desatava:
> el diablo antiguo en esto s' travajava,
> por fer mal a cristianos nunca en al andava.
>
> (s. 70)

> Quando ovo rey Rodrigo sus poderes juntados,
> era poder sin guisa mas todos desarmados;
> lidiar fueron con moros, levaron sus pecados,
> ca fue de los profetas esto profetizado.
>
> (s. 77)

> Era la cosa puesta e de Dios otorgada
> que serian los d' España metidos a espada,

> a los dueños primeros les seria tomada;
> tornaron en el canpo ellos otra vegada.
> Cuidavan los cristianos ser bien asegurados,
> que avian a los moros en el canpo rancados;
> fueran se los paganos essas oras tornados,
> si non por quien non ayan perdon de sus pecados.
>
> (ss. 80-81)

One of the most important preludes to the central—and cyclical—segment of the poem is the underlining of Spain's own "Babylonian" captivity beginning with stanza 89. Again the poet dwells on the triumph of sin—not so much the sin of which the Moors are only generally guilty, but specifically and insistently the sin of the Christians:

> Dezian los mal fadados: "en mal ora nasçimos:
> diera nos Dios España, guardar non la sopimos,
> si en grand coita somos nos bien lo meresçimos,
> por nuestro mal sentido en grand yerro caimos.
>
> (s. 98)
> Nos a Dios falesçiendo a nos el fallesçido,
> lo que otros ganaron emos lo nos perdido,
> partiendo nos de Dios a se de nos partido,
> tod el bien de los godos por end es confondido."
> Diera Dios essas oras grand poder al pecado,
>
> (ss. 100-101a)

This portion of the poem concludes with a long "oración de los fugitivos" in which some of the most common figural segments are evoked in a grand hodgepodge to refer to the plight of the Goths, the love for liberation, and their now objectified sinful state (ss. 107-13).

In the remaining stanzas of the prelude to Fernán González's role in this mythic-figural history of Castile, the poet continues with the history of the Gothic-Castilian kings, arriving finally to the birth, maturity, and realization of the mission of Fernán González. [28]

Parts 2-4, stanzas 191-585, are essentially cyclical and repetitive in terms of the meaning which the poet assigns to the broad

---

[28] Before turning to the central segment of his work, the poet reiterates the importance of Castile (ss. 171-73) and previews the role of Fernán González in her liberation from captivity (ss. 174-76).

panorama of historical events. The most obvious "higher" meaning assignable to the narration is that which emphasizes the encounter with the Moors (parts 2 and 4) and the struggle to liberate Castile from their dominion. As Armistead has pointed out,[29] the *Poema* is conceived within the framework of a holy war with far-reaching religious implications. Certainly in its cyclical stressing of this aspect, the *Poema de Fernán González* is the best example in Spanish medieval poetry of a well thought-out elaboration of the figural motif of a holy war struggle between forces of good and evil. This struggle is most vividly brought out in an important series of significantly "antihistorical" events in part 4: the encounter with the Moors. It is an encounter which lasts the figurative three days and culminates in the final liberation-resurrection of the Christians.[30]

---

[29] "El monje de Arlanza, lleno de entusiasmo reconquistador, deseaba ver, hasta en la dominación de Hispania por los godos, una guerra santa contra el Islám, trasunto de empresas hispano-cristianas en tiempos muy posteriores. De ahí que se introduzca, que se deslice en el texto la alusión, fugaz e inverosímil, a unos moros pre-góticos, seres míticos y a la vez íntimamente relacionadas con la actualidad del poeta y su personal perspectiva histórica" (pp. 16-17). Armistead is here referring to the conquest of the Peninsula referred to above, particularly to s. 59d "(¡mal grado a los moros que la solían tener!)." Armistead has made many revealing observations on the idiosyncratic personal historical perspective, but without being able to place them within the context of the figural structural motif, a motif which I believe underlies, organizes, and explains to us just why the poet's point of view is so idiosyncratically antihistorical—precisely, of course, because his interest is in "poetic" not "historic" meaning.

[30] For the importance of the triple pattern, consider J. P. Keller's two revealing schemata of the *Poema* (pp. 236-37). The first deals with the general organization of the work:

I. Spain before Fernán González.
    A. Gothic Kings.
    B. Conquest by Moslems.
    C. Reconquest to advent of Fernán González.
II. Establishment of hero's supremacy over Moslems and Navarre.
    A. First battle against Moslems.
    B. First battle against Navarre.
    C. Second battle against Moslems.
III. Liberation of Castile from León.
    A. Cortes in León; capture and imprisonment in Navarrese jail; release by and marriage to Sancha.
    B. Second battle against Navarre with capture and imprisonment of García Sánchez and release through intervention of Sancha; third battle against Moslems; third battle against Navarre.

A well-defined trajectory is operant here. The poet chooses to present a figure of evil which not only historically precedes the savior figure of good but also allows the poet to emphasize the frightening qualities of evil as it intimidates the men and awakens their courage. This figure of evil is presented as a serpent, thus coordinating directly with the earliest figure of Satan's forces—the serpent of the Garden of Eden. Here it appears in the Eden which is Spain struggling to extirpate the roots of perdition and captivity from its soil:

> Vieron aquella noche una muy fiera cosa:
> venie por el aire una sierpe rabiosa,
> dando muy fuertes gritos la fantasma astrosa,
> toda venie sangrienta, bermeja commo rosa.
> Fazia ella senblante que ferida venia,
> semejava en los gritos que el çielo partia,
> alunbrava las uestes el fuego que vertia:
> todos ovieron miedo que quemar los venia.
>
> (ss. 471-72)

> Quando gelo contaron assi commo lo vieron,
> entendio bien el conde que grand miedo ovieron,
> que esta atal figura diablos la fizieron,
> a los pueblos cruzados revolver los quisieron.
>
> (s. 476)

C.   Cortes in León, imprisonment, release by Sancha; negotiations over debt; liberation of Castile from León.

It is no accident that the dominant figural motifs are to be found in the second, central portion of the work, one segment of which Keller expands as follows to underline the all-pervasive tripartite organization:

II.   Establishment of hero's supremacy over Moslems and Navarre.
    A.   First battle against Moslems.
        1.   Events leading to battle.
            a.   Capture of Carazo by Fernán González; anger of Almanzor; approach of Moslem army.
            b.   Discussion of Castilians as to whether to fight.
            c.   Hunt and prophecy episode.
        2.   Battle.
            a.   Rider and steed engulfed by chasm.
            b.   Fighting up to Almanzor's tent.
            c.   Anger and flight of Almanzor.
        3.   Events after battle.
            a.   Pursuit.
            b.   Collection of booty from battlefield.
            c.   Gifts to San Pedro de Arlanza.

"... Algun moro astroso que sabe encantar,
fizo aquel diablo en sierpe figurar,
por amor que podiesse a vos mal espantar,
con este tal engaño cuidando nos torvar.

Commo sodes sesudos bien pododes saber
que el non ha poder de mal a nos fazer,
ca tollo le don Cristo el su fuerte poder,
veades que son locos los quel quieren creer.

Que es de tod el mundo en uno el poder,
que a el sol devemos todos obedeçer,
ca el es poderoso de dar e de toller:
atal Señor com este devemos nos temer.

Quien este Señor dexa e en la bestia fia,
tengo que es caido a Dios en muy grand ira,
anda en fallimiento la su alma mesquina:
quantos que assi andan el diablo los guia.

Tornemos en lo al que agora estamos,
trabajando avemos, mester es que duramos,
con ellos en el canpo cras mañana seamos,
todos en su logar assi commo mandamos."

(ss. 482-86)

The Count immediately interprets the serpent as an attempt at
deceit by a Moorish astrologer, an indication of the concrete embodiment of evil in the non-Christian invaders. [31] It is in the spirit

---

[31] In part three, however, the Navarrese, although nominally Christian,
personify the forces of evil (s. 294). Thus the superpatriotic poet affirms
once again the synthesis of political and religious cosmic importance assigned
to Castile in his *Poema*. Nevertheless, Castile's troubles with Navarre are due
also to the basic sinfulness of man, a sinfulness which must be conquered
in its personification as a challenging attacker (ss. 323-24). Fernán González's
wound described in this passage reveals a casual and rather gratuitous reference of Christ. Finally, as the Count again must rally his men, he attempts
to inspire them while at the same time "unconsciously" providing for the
poet a vehicle for reaffirming, in the mention of some major figural person-
alities, the far-reaching intent of his narrative framework:

"... Non cuentan d' Alexandre las noches nin los dias,
cuentan sus buenos fechos e sus cavallerias;
cuentan del rey Davit que mato a Golias,
de Judas Macabeo fijo de Matatias.

Carlos e Valdovinos, Roldan e don Ojero,
Terrin e Gualdabuey, Arnald e Olivero,
Torpin e don Rinaldos e el gascon Angelero,
Estol e Salomon, otro su compañero.

Estos e otros muchos que non vos he nonbrados,
por lo que ellos fizieron seran sienpre ementados;

of this same narrative (and historical) correlation that Fernán González stresses the false power of the non-Christian, against which he means to rival the true power of the world—that of the Lord— embodied in the only person able to realize an exegesis of the signs which the troops have seen (cf. s. 520a: "El conde don Fernando, mas bravo que serpiente").

At this point, as at repeated previous moments in the narrative of the Castilians' confrontation with the satanic forces from without (the Moors of Menéndez Pidal's parts 2 and 4; Keller's IIA and IIC) and from within (Menéndez Pidal's part 3; Keller's IIB), Fernán González's men weaken in courage and spirit, condemn the Count's forceful leadership, and must in turn be reinspired in their mission by the indefatigable warrior. However, in this instance, Fernán González's own spiritual turmoil in the face of the demands put upon him by himself and by his Lord is revealingly highlighted by the poet:

> Era en fuerte cuita el conde don Fernando,
> iva, si se l' fiziesse, su muerte aguisando;
> alço suso los ojos, al Criador rogando,
> com si sovies con el assi le esta llamando:
>
> (s. 551)

> "... Padre, Señor del mundo, e vero Jesucriste,
> de lo que me dixeron nada non me toviste:
> que me acorrerias comigo lo posiste,
> yo non te fallesçiendo ¿por que me fallesçiste?
> Señor, pues es el conde de ti desanparado,
> que por alguna culpa eres del despagado,
> resçibe tu, Señor, en guarda est condado:
> si non, sera aina por suelo astragado.
>
> (ss. 555-56)

> Todos los mis vassallos que aqui son finados
> serian por su señor este dia vengados,

> si tan buenos non fueran oy serien olvidados,
> seran los buenos fechos fasta la fin contados.
> Por tanto ha mester que los dias contemos,
> los dias e las noches en que los espendemos,
> quantos en valde passan nunca los cobraremos,
> amigos, bien lo vedes que mal seso fazemos."
>
> (ss. 357-60)

todos en paraiso conmigo ayuntados:
faria muy grande honra el cond a sus criados."

(s. 559)

Fernán González's lament is obviously a frank accommodation of Christ's lament on the cross, "Why hast Thou forsaken me?" Both Jesus, the primary Savior, and the neo-Christ figure incarnated in the Count, secondary savior of the highly symbolic Castilian Christian political autonomy, arrive at a crossroads in their mission when they must exteriorize their inner turmoil over the clearly unsympathetic course which events are taking. In both cases, nevertheless, the agony is temporary and serves as a catharsis by which the vision is cleared and the path to be followed that much more defined. In the case of Fernán González, his immediate recovery and reaffirmation of mission are evident, as he, again echoing Christ's words, promises eternal salvation for his men.

In order for the figural trajectory to reach its mature culmination, the poet must juxtapose upon the apparition of the figure of evil an equally impressive—but more genuine—apparition of a figure of grace and salvation. This he accomplishes with a vision of Santiago (to whom Fernán González stands in a natural figural relationship as a flesh-and-blood realization of the principles which the saint represents). The Santiago episode is intended for direct comparison in wording and effect with the appearance of the serpent:

> Fueron contra los moros, las azes bien paradas:
> nunca vio omne nado gentes tan esforçadas;
> el moro Almançor con todas sus mesnadas,
> con ellos fueron luego fuerte miente enbargadas.
> Veien d' una señal tantos pueblos armados,
> ovieron muy grand miedo, fueron mal espantados;
> de qual parte venian eran maravillados:
> lo que mas les pesava que eran todos cruzados.
> Dixo rey Almançor: "Esto non puede ser;
> ¿Do l' recreçio al conde atan fuerte poder?
> Cuidava yo oy sin duda le matar o prender,
> e avra con sus gentes el a nos cometer."

(ss. 562-64)

Here the audience of the poem requires no exegesis from a superior point of view. Santiago is clearly a triumphant figural contrast to the serpent. He strikes fear and defeat in the Moorish troops because he embodies the true powers of the righteousness of his holy war which the Castilian warrior possesses by direct inspiration. The discordance of the *ex machina* fabrication of the two apparitions is best understood within the context of the otherwise highly naturalistic portrayal of the confrontations of war. The apparitions are rhetorical devices which provide a concrete correlation of the religious and moral abstractions that inform the very basic action of the *Poema*. That abstractions are insisted on over and over in the cyclical organization of the poem is important in the effort to understand the gross and flagrant violations of historical fact which have so often been the concern—and consternation—of the critic. In the final encounter with the Moors, which is successful on the third day when the Christians rout the enemy, the poet has elaborated the most extravagant examples of his figural motif. It is an elaboration which culminates not only the trajectory of parts 2, 3, and 4, but of the whole *Poema* as well. Castile's resurrection and liberation from captivity has at long last been effected. The episodes which fill the last 150 stanzas of the work are but variations on a theme, as the poet presents essentially further combinations of the pattern "Castile threatened—the Count troubled—the troops rallied —Castile's independence reaffirmed." As a denouement, these episodes strike the reader as rather weak and can only be justified when examined against the dynamic cyclical scheme which lends the *Poema* its strongest unity. It is not accidental that the closing words of the poet in what we have of the manuscript seem conclusive in their reiteration of what has been, after all, the whole point of the poem—its elaboration of the figure of Fernán González:

> Assaz eran navarros caveros esforçados,
> que en qualquier lugar serian buenos provados,
> omnes son de grand cuenta, de coraçon loçanos:
> mas eran contra 'l conde todos desventurados.
> Quiso Dios al buen conde esta graçia fazer,
> que moros nin cristianos non le podian vencer.
>
> (ss. 767-68b)

The Count from the very outset of his role in the reconquest is conscious first of his relation to the Christian values associated with the figure of the Son of Man, and second to his mission in the redemption and deliverance from captivity of Castile (see his af-

firmation to his men on the role of the individual in the defeat
of the Moors, ss. 217-24). During a time when, as the clichés of
literary history tell us, the emphasis is upon the "history of the
universe," the particularized *Poema de Fernán González* chooses
to exalt a readily identifiable and quasi-historic figure as the dynamic
force of the composition. In the last analysis, Fernán González,
like the Son of Man he emulates, participates in the grand drama
of human (Christian) destiny—yet both men are willing subjects of
the design as well as dynamic principles. Thus the Count is always
presented within the framework not only of standard figural symbolism but also of the particular concept of Castilian sin and redemption
held by the thirteenth-century poet.

One of the basic ironic situations presented repeatedly by the
work is the pattern of the men's disillusionment and encouragement
by their leader, who suffers his own private discouragement (cf.
s. 232) and is sustained by various prophecies and visions, [32] and
their eventual reaffirmation of mission. Like Christ, Fernán González must sustain in the minds of a weak, sinful, and distrusting
following the promise of his transcendent purpose, continually re-
interpreting as signs of hope what to others are signs of despair:

> Uno de los del conde, valiente cavallero,
> cavalgaua un cavallo, fermoso e ligero,
> puso l' de las espuelas por cima d' un otero,
> abrio s' con el la tierra e somio se el cavero.
> Todos desta señal fueron muy espantados:
> "Esto que conteçio fue por nuestros pecados;
> bien semeja que Dios nos a desanparados,
> mejor seso fizieramos si fueramos tornados.
> Sin ferida nenguna Dios nos quiere matar,
> contra Dios non podemos sin daño pelear;
> bien lo vemos que quiere a moros ayudar,
> ¿e como nos podriamos contra ellos lidiar?"
> "Amigos", dixo 'l conde, "¿com assi desmayades?
> Ganar mal prez por sienpre en poco non querades;
> de gallinas semeja que el coraçon ayades,
> ca sin nulla ferida covardia mostrades.

---

[32] Like everything else in the *Poema* the prophecies and visions are
threefold. Keller analyzes them in detail to explain their structure on the
basis of the symbolic tripartite pattern.

> Lo que este signo muestra quiero vos departir,
> com' a de ser sin dubda vos entiendo dezir:
> la tierra dura e fuerte vos fazedes somir,
> pues ¿quales otras cosas a vos podran sofrir?
> Ellos non valen nada por contra vos seer,
> et vuestros coraçones veo enflaquescer.
> Por esto non devedes ningun miedo aver
> ca yo aqueste dia cobdiciava veer.
> Amigos, d' una cosa so yo bien sabidor:
> ellos seran vençidos, ho sere vençedor;
> en grand afruenta en canpo seré con Almoçor,
> vere los castellanos com guardades senor."
>
> (ss. 256-62)

The poet leaves little doubt as to how we are to interpret the post-New Law Fernán González and Almozor, as he evokes the pre-New Law figures, respectively, of Christ and Satan:

> Por non vos detener en otras ledanias,
> fue Almozor vençido con sus cavallerias:
> alli fue demostrado el poder del Mexias,
> el conde fue David e Almozor Golias.
>
> (s. 272)

The major ironic motif of the Count as the Savior to both his men and his homeland is reiterated in part 3 (ss. 322-23; 340-42), where the Navarrese represent the satanic anti-Christ, and again in part 4 (s. 391; 397-405; 423-26), where the Moors threaten for the second time. It is obvious that this ironic motif has an overwhelming pertinency to the poem's major figural motif of fall and redemption. The poet is insistent in seeing the entire narrative in terms of the Lord's design:

> Dixo m' que mal fazia por tanto que tardava
> a aquel Rey de los reyes por cuya amor lidiava,
> que fuesse e non tardasse contra la gent pagana,
> que ¿por que avia miedo pues que el me ayudava?
>
> (s. 433)

Any cowardice in the men is repeatedly put in the broader terms of the betrayal of Judas:

"... Todo aquel de vos que del canpo saliere,
o con miedo de muerte a presion de les diere,
quede por alevoso qui tal fecho fiziere,
con Judas en infierno yaga quando moriere."
Quando esto oyo el su pueblo loçano,
todos por una boca fablaron muy priado:
"Señor, lo que tu dizes es de nos otorgado,
qui fuyer de nos yaga con Judas abraçado."

(ss. 450-51)

In summary, then, despite any marginal interests of the *Poema de Fernán González* and despite the manuscript imperfections of the concluding segments, a reading of the work in terms of a discoverable underlying motif reveals not only the poet's dependence on an all-pervasive sacramental numerical organization, but his allegiance to a unique and peculiar concept of Castiliart history and importance derived from the widely diffused figural design. El Conde Fernán González, both Adam figure and Christ figure, is the dynamic principle of this design, a design which the poet intricately weaves into a cyclical pattern affirming his patriotic vision.

That the *Poema* is far from an exceptional work of art is no bold evaluation; J. P. Keller's own feeling is that it suffers from the insupportable weight of its symbolic structure. Nevertheless, with the earlier *Poema de Mio Cid* and the later *Libro de buen amor* it shares the distinction of being one of the most conscientiously elaborated examples of medieval Spanish poetry. [33]

The works examined up to this point have utilized to a certain extent the concept of the history of mankind as an ordered realization of a divine plan. Man becomes aware of the plan through the signs of prophecy, prefiguration, and fulfillment which have been revealed to him by a God who wishes man to understand his law and the destiny of mankind. Medieval historiography is based in great part on the concept of the seven epochs of the universe.

---

[33] No far-reaching analysis of structure has yet been done for the *Libro de buen amor*. Concerning the structure of the *Cid*, see Edmund de Chasca, *Estructura y forma en el "Poema de Mio Cid"* (Iowa City, Iowa, 1956); as well as Gustavo Correa's review article, "*Estructura y forma en el Poema de Mio Cid*," *Hispanic Review* 25 (1957): 280-90. De Chasca's work has been recently revised as *El arte juglaresco en el "Poema de Mio Cid"* (Madrid, 1967).

(Seven was a frequent numerical symbol for completeness and finality and also corresponds to the time required for the creation, on the seventh day of which God had completed his task and rested.) St. Augustine's division in the *City of God* may be taken as a typical example of these seven divisions of history: "1) Adam to the Flood, 2) the Flood to the Tower of Babel, 3) Abraham to David, 4) David to the Babylonish Captivity, 5) the Babylonish Captivity to the Crucifixion, 6) the Crucifixion to the Last Judgment, and, finally, 7) an eternal sabbath with the damned in hell, the saved in paradise, and this earth uninhabited. In all ages, God punishes the evil and rewards the good." [34]

Unfortunately, it is not until the sixteenth century, well after what we can call the Middle Ages, that Spain produces a work with such a broad, panoramic perspective. Such a work is Gil Vicente's *Auto da História de Deus* (first performed in 1527). [35] Although a little later than the majority of the works analyzed in this study, Vicente's *auto* is worthy of attention for its elaboration of a "history of God" wherein every man is a figure of Christ, as well as for its importance as an example of figural literature during the Renaissance. The exordium given by an angel makes clear the broad historical sweep of the work:

> Ainda que todalas cousas passadas
> sejam notórias a Vossas Altezas,
> a história de Deus tem tais profundezas,
> que nunca se perdem serem recontadas.
> E porque o tenor
> da resurreição de nosso Senhor
> tem as raízes naquelle pomar,
> ao pé, d'aquella árvore que ouvistes contar,

---

[34] As quoted in Frederick B. Artz, *The Mind of the Middle Ages*, 3d ed. (New York, 1958), pp. 83-84.

[35] My text is from the *Obras completas*, 6 vols. (Lisbon, 1959), 2: 171-215. Many of Vicente's other *autos* also make use of figural references. In many cases, however, there is a note of *commedia dell'arte* which detracts to a considerable degree from any serious religious intent which they may have. The *Auto da História de Deus*, although markedly Renaissance in style, has borrowed its theme and the elaboration of the theme from the medieval figural literature, and it is therefore more pertinent than others of the *autos*. In addition, many of the *autos* are purely allegorical in a Hellenistic sense, a characteristic which is also evident in the *auto* discussed here (cf. *O Mundo, O Tempo, A Morte*).

aonde Adão se fez pecador,
convém se lembrar. ...
Agora vereis
o que por diversos doctores lereis
d'*ab initio mundi* até à resurreição;
à qual se endereça a final tenção
dos versos seguintes. ...

(pp. 171-72)

The first segment of the work deals with the resentment of the agents of hell toward the Garden of Eden and the idea that Adam and Eve will be accorded the grace denied the fallen angels. Characteristically, it is Lucifer who perpetrates the scheme to bring about the fall of Adam and Eve. [36] He advises Satan:

Faze-te cobra, por dissimular,
porque pareças do mesmo pomar,
que sabes das frutas as graças que tem;
porque hás-de dizer:
senhora fermosa, deveis de saber
que aquela fruta que vos foi vedada
oh! quanta ciência em si tem cerrada.

(pp. 174-75)

Lucifer is cast here into a complex role. On the one hand, he is the figure of sin, the epitome of the unholy forces of the universe. As such he is antithetical to St. Michael, the archangel, the prototype of virtue for mankind which he is often beseeched in prayer to defend. However, Lucifer is also a figure of sinful man—it is he who suggests the apple to Satan (the dualistic antithesis of God) as the appropriate means for deceiving Adam and Eve. When the pair accept the temptation of the devil they will have fulfilled the prefigurement of the fall of mankind inherent in the fall of the angels. Until mankind's resurrection through the Coming of Christ, Everyman will be in one sense the fulfillment of Lucifer's design.

The apple, the means proposed by Lucifer to deceive Adam and Eve, is one of the most frequent symbols in figural art and literature.

---

[36] See in passing J. P. W. Crawford, "The Devil as a Dramatic Figure in the Spanish Religious Drama before Lope de Vega," *Romanic Review* 1 (1910): 302-12, 374-83.

With reference to Adam, it symbolizes mankind's fall into sin through his acceptance of the devil's temptation to challenge the Lord. In this sense, the apple looks backward to man's relationship with the sinful legions of the universe. In another sense, however, the apple bespeaks the salvation of man and his resurrection from sin. Adam, in accepting the apple, took upon himself the burden of the sins of mankind in prefiguration of the way in which Christ—the new Adam and the fulfillment of the Adam figure—will also accept the burden of sin and will offer himself up in sacrifice for the restoration to grace of mankind. [37] Thus, Lucifer's words, "quanta ciência em ti tem cerrada," call our attention to the way in which the apple —and the events associated with it—are central to the Christian concept of history. [38]

An important theme iterated by Vicente's *auto* is the struggle between sin and grace as the unifying motif of history. Vicente eschews the possibility of making Satan and Lucifer into pale spokesmen for the fall of man when he accords them an importance worthy of their role as one of the principal motivating forces of the story of sinful man. Thus, Lucifer acknowledges that Adam will not be simply the victim of the serpent's temptation, but that Satan will only capitalize on Adam's free will to sin:

> Onde força há perdemos direito;
> que o fino pecado há-de ser de vontade,
> formando desprezo contra a Majestade;
> e não serão nossos, se for doutro jeito.
>
> (p. 176)

Ultimately, man shares the burden of guilt for his fall, and, as the participant in the events which will lead to his redemption, he is not the victim of God's plan, but rather the penitent recipient of his mercy. Vicente, in dwelling on the concept of free will, introduces the theme of the *sic et non*—man's potential for grace as well as

---

[37] In the second *auto* edited by Florence Whyte, "Three *Autos* of Jorge de Montemayor," *PMLA* 43 (1928): 953-89, the poet presents Adam's benefit to mankind in general and theme of man delighted at God's having taken his form: "Dichoso Adam ..." (vv. 31-50). The third *auto* is similar in theme.

[38] Gonzalo de Berceo, in the introduction to the *Milagros*, discusses the figural relationship between the tree of the apple and the tree of the cross.

sin.[39] The nature of mankind is sinful by virtue of Adam's fall and his acceptance of the original sin which is the heritage of mankind. However, since man is made in the image of the Lord, since Everyman is an Adam figure, he also bears in him the desire for grace and the hope of salvation through the Coming of Christ. Man's sinful nature is usually spoken of symbolically as his prison, and the collective imprisonment of mankind before the Coming of Christ is characterized by the limbo of Christian doctrine. Vicente's *auto* makes use of these ramifications of the introduction of the *sic et non*.

The second segment of the work introduces several allegorical personifications whose function it is to present the period of the Old Testament and the various prefigurements of the New Law. An angel explains:

> *Deus, cui proprium est miserere,*
> porque o seu próprio é perdoar
> de todo a sanha não quer executar,
> e a suma bondade assim lh'o requere.
> ... E porque o pecado é em si temporal,
> e a bondade de Deus é infinda,
> procede em grandeza a toda cousa finda,
> e ser poderoso é seu natural.
> ... E a ti porém
> manda-te, Tempo, que temperes bem
> este relógio, que te dou, das vidas;
> e como as horas forem compridas
> de que fez mercê à vida d'alquém,
> serão despedidas.

> (pp. 179-80)

Central to an understanding of God's plan is the concept of time as a function of his disposition of men and events. In due time man will be saved and in due time he will know the mystery of God's universe. Adam and Eve appear to converse on their fate. Victims of Time, they must live in the World, which thrives on their cares, confronted with Death, the "fruit of their sin" (pp. 181-84). As Adam goes off to work by the sweat of his brow, *O Mundo* introduces Abel, the first of the major prefigurements of Christ:

---

[39] See passim. Otis Green, *Spain and the Western Tradition* (Madison, Wis., 1963-1966), "Sic et Non," pp. 15-16.

64 CHRISTIAN ALLEGORY

> *Mun.* Ora venha Abel seu filho carnal [de Adão]
> e não façais conta aqui de Caim,
> que como o homem é homem ruim,
> pera que é dele fazer cabedal?
> Abel é pastor
> amigo de Deus e bom servidor,
> por isso lhe crecem a olho seu gados
>
> *Tem.* Pois porque tem dias tão abreviados?
>
> *Mun.* São fundos segredos que tem o Senhor
> para si guardados.
>
> (pp. 184-85)

Through the use of silence on a subject, Abel is introduced along
with reference to Cain, the figure of man as the "homem ruim"
who will kill the Son of Man. Vicente presents Abel as the victim
of his father's sin and as the prisoner of Time and Death:

> *Tem.* Despachai Abel, parti pola fria,
> que já vossas horas estão consumidas.
>
> *Abe.* Ó Tempo, tão curtas são aqui as vidas?
> Senhor, agravais-me, que ainda crecia;
> não há aqui justiça.
> Leixai-me, Morte.
>
> (p. 187)

Abel is cast into the darkness of limbo, where he bemoans his
fate as a man. Man must await the time of his resurrection. The
next figure presented, Job, explains his faith in the covenant of
the Lord:

> Eu creio, Mundo, que o meu Redentor
> vive, e no dia mais derradeiro
> eu o verei Redentor verdadeiro,
> meu Deus, meu Senhor e meu Salvador.
> Eu o verei, eu,
> não outrem por mim, nem com olho seu,
> mas o meu olho, assim como está;
> porque minha carne se levantará,
> e em carne mea verei o Deus meu
> que me salvara.
>
> (p. 191)

Throughout the presentation of the Old Testament figures, Satan, Lucifer, and Belial appear frequently to taunt them and to attempt to weaken their faith in the promise of their salvation and the triumph of God. Although Satan does not succeed in inspiring doubt in Job, he reminds him that he is cursed with the stain of sin. Satan touches Job, who, covered with leprosy, cries out to God:

> Oh chagado de mi, que esta é outra demanda!
> Oh Deus meu! e porque me persegues?
> Contra mim perfias,
> sabendo que nada são os meus dias!
> Minha alma s'enoja já de minha vida,
> e como a seta é minha partida.
> Senhor, meu Senhor! porque te desvias
> de tua guarida?
>
> (p. 192)

In words reminiscent of Christ's agony, Job's lament reiterates the despair of man deprived of the comfort of the Lord's presence and the cleansing power of his son's grace.

The World again appears to mark the transition from the four prebiblical figures, Adam, Eve, Abel, and Job, to four scriptural prophets, Moses, Isaiah, David, and Abraham—all prefigurements of Christ. Each one speaks in turn, relating some aspect of God's revelation and man's understanding of and faith in the divine figures. Moses proclaims:

> E assentarei
> mistérios profundos no livro da lei,
> tudo figuras da Sancta Trindade,
> tudo mistérios da eternidade,
> que Deus me dirá e eu escreverei
> à sua vontade.
>   E ele estará em pessoa comigo
> aos cinco livros, quando os escrever;
> porque as cerimónias que mandar fazer,
> outras maiores trazerá consigo.
> Tu, homem, penetra,
> e dos sacrifícios não tomes a letra;
> que outro sacrifício figuram em si,
> que matar bezerros, nem aves ali:
> outra mais alta oferta soltera,
> e outro Genesi.
>
> (pp. 196-97)

Moses emphasizes the most common procedure employed by Christianity in seeing the truth of its revelation inherent in the older law of former men and events. Vicente's drama is anachronistic in the same sense as the *Auto de los Reyes Magos*. The three wise men and Moses are given an auto-commentary quite disconsonant with their true historical roles. Yet, from the Christian point of view, in both works they are simply made to articulate a meaning for themselves which the exegete felt secure in assigning to them. The artificiality of their exaggerated self-awareness was not looked upon as marring in any way the "truth" of their utterances. And, to the degree that the *História de Deus* is a summary of that history up to a particular point (that is, up to the sixth epoch of the New Testament), all of previous history is easily portrayed and accommodated in terms of a resolution of God's design and the dispersion of any doubt as to the meaning of his figures. The audience, of course, observed this parade of figures and personifications with a comfort arising from an intimate awareness of the only possible answer to Job's lamentation.

When the four prophets have spoken, *O Mundo* again appears to mark the transition to the fourth part of the work. We have heard Adam of the first epoch; Moses, Abraham, and David of the second, third, and fourth epochs, respectively. The last great figure of Christ, Saint John the Baptist of the fifth epoch, is now introduced:

> De lei de Escritura e lei natural
> já temos passados os mais principais;
> venha a lei de graça, porque os mortais
> alcancem a glória de sempre eternal.
> Venha o primeiro
> glorioso Joannes, santo pregoeiro,
> santo sem mágoa de Deus enviado,
> santo nacido e santificado,
> mostrando às gentes alto cordeiro,
> com muito cuidado.
>
> (p. 200)

John proclaims the Coming of Christ and the manner in which he will bring redemption to mankind. Vicente draws upon one of the common symbols of the resurrection, the "ave phoenix" of the bestiaries, to epitomize Christ's resurrection. As before, John's utterances are punctuated by the appearance of the omnipresent Satan. John concludes with the assuring words "ecce agnus Dei," whereupon Time appears with his clock, the clock which has marked the unfolding of God's design in its relentless realization and revelation:

> Este relógio é muito forte,
> vós perdoai-me, Senhor San João,
> que vossas horas cumpridas estão,
> segundo buscastes tão cedo a morte,
> e por vossa vontade.
> Vós não quereis senão pregar verdade,
> e ela vos leva da vida presente.
>
> (p. 203)

Thus, John, like all men, has a specific and well-defined role in history. His appearance on the stage and his brief contribution to the development of the play correspond to his integral but temporal role in the divine plan. He has spoken his part, fulfilled his figural role, and he must cede his place to the next component of God's drama. John is cast into limbo, the prison of the soul, and a *romance* in Castilian describes mankind's lament and beseeches the Virgin to bring forth the Holy Child.

The final segment of the *História de Deus,* corresponding to the sixth epoch, introduces the figure of Adam and his descendents who appear to detail their sinful plight and their faithful trust in an eventual salvation. Again it is the World, our consciousness of God's history, which introduces the Savior. Christ tells man the reason for his coming and the manner in which he is to redeem the sinner. Time interrupts to emphasize that the chain of events instituted by Adam's fall has reached a certain resolution:

> Meu Senhor, eu que farei?
> no relógio que me destes
> digo qu'inda que nascestes
> não se entende em vós a lei,
> pois que vós mesmo a fizestes.
>
> (pp. 208-209)

Christ replies:

> *Modicum videbitis me,*
> eu a cumprirei, que a fiz;

porque o rei que é bom juiz,
como a lei feita é,
faz aquilo que ela diz.
Cedo me despejarás,
tem tu o relógio certo;
em tanto vou-me ao deserto,
e veremos Satanás
se me fala descoberto.

(p. 209)

The remainder of the drama portrays Christ's confrontations with Satan and his followers. Vicente focuses on the way in which Christ brings not only the redemption of mankind and the fulfillment of his prefigurements but also the defeat of Satan:

Chr.   Eis aqui subimos a Hierusalem
        pera tirar o vestido em que ando;
        porque os açoutes me estão esperando.
        Cumpra-se todo o meu mal e meu bem.

(pp. 213-14)

The work concludes with the representation of the crucified Christ and the release of the souls in limbo, thereby demonstrating definitively the fulfillment of the prophecy of the Lord. [40]

História de Deus is extremely detailed in its portrayal of the major trajectory of the Christian concept of history. In great part, the unity of the drama derives from the use of the allegorical personifications of Time, the World, and Death as agents in God's design. It is particularly Time and the World which serve to integrate into one unified whole the pattern of figural history, emphasizing as they do the reality of the world as the patent symbol of man's fall, and time as the function of his awareness of the unfolding revelation of his God and Christ. [41]

---

[40] Two other sixteenth-century plays, although lacking the sweeping perspective of Vicente's *auto*, dealt with the fulfillment of the divine plan in particularly interesting ways. In J. P. W. Crawford, "*Comedia a lo pastoril para la noche de Navidad:* A Spanish Religious Play of the Sixteenth Century," *Revue hispanique* 24 (1911): 497-541, the poet presents within a framework of personification the conflict between the four virtues over the propriety of the Lord's promise to Adam.

[41] In the introduction, T. R. Hart's interpretation of the "Conde Arnaldos" was rejected as representing an essentially different attitude toward literature

and patristic allegory from the present study. However, Hart's "Gil Vicente's *Auto de la Sibila Cassandra,*" *Hispanic Review* 26 (1958): 35-51, is closer to the problem of the elaboration in a work of literature of the figural motif. Apparently, Hart is not concerned with the perhaps overly subtle distinction which I am making between certain works involving certain structural motifs and the reading of all works from the point of view of a particular interpretational framework for medieval literature. The only reservation which I would have concerning Hart's excellent paper on Vicente is that he adheres basically to the practice of allegory, where the *sententia* is overemphasized at the expense of the *sensus,* as opposed to the practice of figural interpretation, where, as I have stressed repeatedly, a correlation is sought by the poet between the equally important immediate *sensus* and the transcendent *sententia.* Nevertheless, Hart and I are quite in agreement over the *Auto de la Sibila Cassandra,* probably because I feel that it is a work which elaborates structurally the figural motif, while the "Conde Arnaldos" is not in any direct sense of the phrase. Nevertheless, I feel that Hart places too much emphasis on a sacramental interpretation of the first, quite distinctly farcical segment of the *auto* in which Salomão and her three aunts attempt to persuade Cassandra to marry Salomão. Hart would see Salomão as the true grace, rejected by Cassandra's selfish vanity and her foolish notion that she is to be the Virgin. The author's own words prefacing his play must also be either taken into account or explained away: "Tracta-se nella da presumpção da Sibilla Cassandra, que, por espírito prophetico soubesse o misterio da encarnação, presumio que ella era a virgem de quem o Senhor havia de nascer. E com esta opinião nunca quis casar" (Gil Vicente, 1: 49-82). The most obviously figural element is contained in the central segment, where the three prophets, Esais, Moyses and Abrahão, attempt to explain to Cassandra that God's divine plan has already explicitly provided for the Virgin and that her foolish notion derives from a headstrong wish rather than from an accurate interpretation of the Lord's figural signs and prophecies. The *auto* concludes with a representation of the fulfillment of his history, thereby demonstrating conclusively to Cassandra her willful error and giving a well-defined structural unity to the composition.

CHAPTER II

THE FIGURE OF ADAM AND MAN AS SAINT AND SINNER

THE THREE TEXTS DISCUSSED IN THIS CHAPTER represent the poets' preoccupation with the role of man as an individual in the divine history of God. Adam, the father of man, has traditionally been seen as two separate but inextricably interwoven figures: Adam as Cain—murderer, betrayer, unrepentant sinner, unable to comprehend the mission of Christ and the promise of redemption—and Adam as Abel—the sacrificial victim, Christ the redeemer, aware of and responsive to his role in the grand design of the universe.

The thirteenth-century *Reyes de Oriente,* while it deals to a certain extent with divine history, focuses on Christ as the redeemer and on his relationship to two individuals, each a separate side of Adam as the figure of a man condemned who is saved by Christ.

The late Judas play is introduced as probably the fullest treatment in pre-Lope dramatic poetry of one of the most dominant figures of the Christian story. Judas is Adam as man damned by the stain of original sin, propelled by the mark of Cain into ever more repulsive deeds, until he is finally led to betray Christ, the Adam-Abel figure, whose incarnation is man's hope for a release from the depths of his sinful nature. Thus, Judas is an important correlative of the story of man, functioning not only to portray man as a sinner but also to fulfill the prophecies for the sinner's redemption.

Our last example is the complex and difficult *Libro de buen amor.* Although Juan Ruiz's poem means many things and explores multiple aspects of the human situation, an attempt will be made to demonstrate that one aspect dealt with by the poet is his commitment to a portrayal of man caught in the web of his dual nature of Adam as saint and sinner.

The anonymous *Libro de los Reyes de Oriente* (ca. 1200), although a nondramatic composition, at first glance appears to take up where the *Auto de los Reyes Magos* leaves off. However, despite that in the opening lines the theme of the former is similar to that of the *Auto*, the figural structure which the *Libro* employs is radically different in terms of organization and development. The work consists of two parts: Herod's interrogation of the three wise men, his order for the massacre of the innocents, and Rachel's lament over the death of her children (vv. 1-79); and the bulk of the narrative, which relates the flight into Egypt, the detainment of the holy family by two thieves, the curing of the son of one of the thieves through immersion in the bath water of Jesus, and the crucifixion of Christ, who is flanked by the sons of the two thieves —the one on his right saved through his cure and repentance, and the other damned by his sins (vv. 80-245). [1]

In the first part of the poem, the author relies for his exposition on two frequent figures: Herod and Rachel. Herod figured prominently in the *Auto de los Reyes Magos* as a type representing the Old Law and the limited power of a temporal king. In this role, his anxiety is one born of a threat to his dominion by a new king whose power and rule far transcend any known by the world before. In the work at hand, Herod is seen more in his role of a Cain figure. [2] Cain's killing of Abel—the favorite of the Lord—functions as the Old Testament prefigurement of Christ's death at the hands of mankind, symbolized by the traitor Judas. Herod's desire to rid himself of the threat to his outdated power prefigures the eventual crucifixion of Christ. The poet presents Herod as the figure of the anti-Christ:

---

[1] My text is from the edition by Manuel Álvar, *Libro de la infancia y muerte de Jesús* (*Libre dels tres reys d'Orient*) (Madrid, 1965).

[2] Another event related to Herod reinforces the understanding of him as a Cain figure. Mark 6 relates the story of the beheading of John the Baptist through the intrigues of Herod. John is usually interpreted as the last of the Old Testament prefigurements of Christ and one of the principal links between Christ and the Old Law.

> Pues muchas vezes oyestes contar
> de los tres Reyes que vinieron buscar
> a Jhesucristo, que era nado,
> vna estrella los guiando;
> et de la grant maravilla
> que les avino en la villa
> do Herodes era el traidor,
> enemigo del Criador.
>
> (vv. 1-8)

In contrast to Herod, Christ is established as the universal king through his acceptance of the offerings of the three wise men. Each offering is intended to reveal one facet of the Savior's dominion:

> Entraron los reys mucho homildosos
> e fincaron los hinojos
> e hobieron gozo por mira:
> ofrecieron oro e ençienso e mirra.
> Baltasar ofreçió oro,
> porque era rey poderoso;
> Melchior mirra, por dulçora,
> por condir la mortal corona,
> E Gaspar le dio ençienso
> que assí era derecho.
>
> (vv. 35-44)

Thus, the Son of God, the fulfillment of the figures of Adam and Abel, is at this time exposed to the threat of Herod, the contemporary Cain figure, who is angered at the prospect of a king more universal than he.

Although the poet does not describe the ensuing massacre of the innocents, he focuses his attention upon Rachel, whose lament is heard in heaven:

> Toda madre puede entender
> cuál duelo podrié seyer,
> que en el çielo fue
> oido el planto de Rachel.
> Dexemos los moçuelos
> e non hayamos d'ellos duelos:
> Por quien fueron martiriados,
> suso al çielo son levados;
> cantarán siempre delante Él,
> en uno con sant Miguel;

La gloria tamaña será
que nunca más fin habrá.

(vv. 68-79)

Rachel and her lament prefigure the lament of the Virgin at the crucifixion of her (innocent) son. The poet develops in the first segment of his poem references in the Old Law which prefigure the eventual death of Christ: Herod, who, although unsuccessful in his search for the Holy Child, articulates the resentment toward Christ which will occasion his crucifixion; and Rachel, whose lament bespeaks the intensely human sorrow of the mother for the lost child, a sorrow which the Virgin will in time experience as her own and as the sorrow of a mankind at the death of its Savior.

While the organization of the first part of the *Libro de los Reyes de Oriente* is simple in its narrative presentation of the events leading up to the flight into Egypt, the second part offers more complex parallels which deviate significantly from the biblical account of the two men who die with Christ. In this sense, the narrative is anticlimactic, since the reader knows and accepts the outcome of the story. Thus, the poet's major concern lies in his development of a closer relationship to Christ for the two thieves than is usually drawn by the traditional accounts.

The poet begins with a description of the family's flight into Egypt, insisting on the written authority for the Angel's command: "Vete pora Egipto / Que asi lo manda el escripto" (vv. 88-89). They are waylaid by two thieves who prey upon pilgrims. One insists that the child be killed, a proposal which horrifies his companion. The latter suggests that they go to his house since it is getting late and the first thief reluctantly agrees. The party is well received by the wife of the generous thief, and the poet immediately points out her reaction to the Christ Child:

¡Dios, qué bien recebidos son
de la mujer d'aquel ladrón! :
a los mayores daba plomaços
e al niño toma en braços
e faziales tanto de plaçer
quanto más le podie fer.

(vv. 129-34)

Our attention is now directed to the parallel between the Virgin and the lowly housewife. The latter begs to be allowed to bathe the child, and Mary grants her permission:

De que el agua hovo asaz caliente,
El niño en braços prende.
Mientre l'baña, al non faz
sino cayer lágrimas por su faz.
La Gloriosa la cataba,
demandól' por qué lloraba:
— "Huéspeda, ¿por qué llorades?
"Non me lo celedes, sí bien hayades."
Ella dixo: "Non lo çelaré, amiga,
"mas queredes que vos diga:
"yo tengo tamaña cueita,
"que querría seyer muerta;
"vn fijuelo que había,
"que parí el otro día,
"afelo allí don jaz gafo
"por mi pecado despugado."
La Gloriosa diz: "Dátmelo, varona,
"yo l'bañaré, que no só ascorosa
"e podedes dezir que en este año
"non puede haber mejor baño".
Fue la madre e prísolo en los braços
a la Gloriosa lo puso en las manos;
la Gloriosa lo metió en el agua
Do bañado era
el rey del cielo e de la tierra.
La vertut fue fecha man a mano,
metiól' gafo sacól' sano.
En el agua fincó todo el mal,
tal lo sacó como un cristal.
cuando la madre vio el fijo guarido
grant alegría ha consigo.
— "Huéspeda en buen día a mi casa viniestes
"que a mi fijo me diestes
"et aquel niño que allá jaz,
"que tales miraglos faz,
"Atal es mi esperança
"que Dios es sines dubdança."

(vv. 154-90)

In this way the diseased son of the "good" thief is cleansed by the purifying waters of the Holy Child's bath. The analogy here with the redemption of the sinner through the cleansing waters of baptism is obvious, and the poor woman's cry of joy and hopeful assurance that the stranger's child is "God without a doubt" reinforce the reader's understanding of this segment of the poem. The woman is sure that her child is diseased because of the sins of the parent—a basic tenet of the concept of original sin. The sickness on the literal level and the original sin on the symbolic level are removed through contact with the Christ Child: a cleansing and a purifying fuse into one act of redemption on the part of him who has fulfilled the promise to man of salvation.

In gratitude for the healing of the thief's child, the holy family is allowed to continue their journey into Egypt, but not until the now-cured child has been commended unto the Holy Child for protection. The poet goes on to relate the birth of a son to the uncharitable thief and how in time both sons, being sons of their fathers, follow in the fathers' footsteps to become thieves who profit from unsuspecting pilgrims. The poet intertwines their fate with that of Jesus and concludes his poem with a suggestion of how we are to understand the relationship of these two men to the Savior:

> e fazian mal atanto
> fasta on los priso Pilato.
> A Iherusalém los aduz,
> mándalos poner en cruz
> En aquel día señalado
> Que Cristus fue crucificado.
> El que en su agua fue bañado,
> fue puesto al su diestro lado;
> luego quel' vio, en él creyó
> e merçet le demandó.
> Nuestro Señor dixo: "Hoy serás comigo
> en el santo paraíso."
> El fi de traidor cuando fablaba
> todo lo despreçiaba.
> Diz: "Varon, ¡cómo eres loco,
> "que Cristus non te valdrá tan poco!
> "A sí non puede prestar
> "¿cómo puede a ti uviar?".
> Este fue en infierno miso
> e el otro en paraísso.
> Dimas fu salvo
> E Gestas fe condampnado.
> Dimas e Gestas,
> medio divina potestas.

(vv. 219-42)

Thus, we see that the thief who dies on the right hand of the Lord is saved, and his companion on the left is damned. That one is saved and the other damned is due not to the nature of their lives, for both were murderous thieves and sinners in the fashion of all men. Rather, Dimas is the sinner who received as a child the saving grace of the Holy Child's presence, and it was this grace which enabled him to beg the mercy of the Lord and to insure his own redemption. [3] In turn and in contrast to their earlier sins manifest in the disease of their son, it was the charity and faith of Dimas's parents which provided him with the basis for his belief in the Lord and his desire for forgiveness and mercy. On the other hand, Gestas has no concept of the mercy of God and is therefore lost forever.

The figural structure of the *Libro de los Reyes de Oriente* is prominent in both sections of the poem. The poet draws an analogy between a series of Adam figures and a series of Cain figures, showing how Christ, as the Son of Man, is the ultimate realization of the figure of Everyman and thus the means of salvation for all the Adams of history. In our poem, Dimas and his father are the two central figures of Adam-Cain as sinful man, who, despite their wicked ways, are afforded salvation through the Coming of Christ and through their ability to understand the way in which Christ is the fulfillment of the prophecy. The words of Dimas's mother are central to the poet's intent:

> "et aquel niño que allá jaz,
> "que tales miraglos faz,
> "atal es mi esperança
> "que Dios es sines dubdança."
>   (vv. 187-90)

The poet presents several Cain figures—men who are incapable of understanding and accepting the divine will: Herod, Gestas and his father, and Pilate (the latter in passing, v. 222). These men lack the necessary charity toward God and his Son, and therefore epitomize the sinful nature of a mankind which destroys its own promise of salvation. The poet reinforces his figural analogies by bringing in two Marian figures: Rachel, a traditional figure of Mary, and the

---

[3] See in regard to this popular Christian concept Tirso de Molina's *El condenado por desconfiado*, where the murderous brigand is saved over the virtuous but doubting man through the former's faith in God's mercy.

mother of Dimas, whose meaning derives from the specific context of the poet's interpretation of the symbolic and figural meaning of the two men who suffer death with Christ. In this way, fewer than 250 lines provide a presentation of the nature of man as a sinner and of his relationship to the Christ Child in terms of the child's forgiveness and salvation. The unity of the work—a work which appears to be composed of two major events lacking any significant inter-relationship—derives from the poet's attempt to fit the traditional story of Herod's anger and the poet's personal account of the two sinful thieves into the same figural framework. [4]

As a paradigmatic sinner, the figure of Judas has long intrigued Christians. [5] Usually considered an Adam-Cain figure, he is presented in his historical role as sinful man unable and/or unwilling to acknowledge the promise of redemption as it is incarnated in the Adam-Abel figure of Christ. Thus, Judas is seen as a member of mankind, a member of the Savior's chosen apostles, underlining vividly that, just as man can be saved and redeemed, he can also ignore and destroy the means for his very salvation. Judas is the embodiment of original sin, bearing externally in Christian symbol-ism the stigma of the fall and the mark of Cain. In treating the *Reyes de Oriente* we have seen how a work of literature can elaborate a balance between man the external sinner and man saved by faith and grace, with the two mediated by the very Christ who forms a bridge between the two aspects of Adam's soul.

Although treated briefly in an early Catalan rhymed legend, [6] the Adam-Cain figure of Judas is not fully represented before the

---

[4] After the writing of this section Margaret Chaplin's study has come to my attention, "The Robbers in the *Libre dels Tres Reys d'Orient*," *Bulletin of Hispanic Studies*, 44 (1967): 88-95. Miss Chaplin is concerned with at-tempting to justify the rather unique treatment in this work of the robber episode, one of the least common of the apocryphal legends surrounding the *Vita Christi*: although she discovers many of the relations discussed in my analysis, her reference to the figural motif would have strengthened considerably her understanding of the unity of the poem, a compact unity which has not been hitherto acknowledged.

[5] See J. E. Gillet, "Traces of the Judas-legend in Spain," *Revue hispa-nique* 65 (1925): 316-41.

[6] "De Judes Escarioth e de la sua vida," in Joan Coronimas, "The Old Catalan Rhymed Legends of the Seville Bible: A Critical Text," *Hispanic Review* 27 (1959): 361-83.

late sixteenth-century *Comedia ... del Nacimiento y Vida de Judas.* [7] Somewhat disparate in its narrative perspective, the work on close examination reveals a guiding interest in presenting Judas as man eternally damned for his original sin.

The play in question follows in detail the major outlines of the Judas legend, as presented by Tyre in his introduction. The first *jornada* of the poem (vv. 1-337), although beginning with a dialogue between the Rrey and Rreyna Elisa, who will adopt Judas after he is set adrift by his father, quickly restores chronology to develop the well-known story of the vision had by Judas's mother (called Zeborea in this version) of the personality which her son will have. Pursuing the issue of the figural interpretation of Judas, the anti-Christ as Adam-Cain, opposed to Christ, the Adam-Abel, this vision is an antitype of the Annunciation:

> ¡O bisión triste y pesado!
> ¡O bisión que no se a oýdo!
> Basta, señor, que he parido
> dormida y con qué cuydado.
> Mas gentil parto se hordena,
> si sale çierto el agüero,
> nazerá nuestro heredero,
> pero para darnos pena.
>
> (vv. 142-49)

> Soñé, señor, que paría
> vn hijo dêsta preñez
> el más malo y más soez
> que significar podría,
> y que por çierto herror
> vn demonio le llebaba
> a vn desierto y le colgaba
> de vn árbol como traydor.
> Demás dêsto que seremos
> por éste de rruin ventura;
> si éste es sueño o desventura
> adelante lo beremos.
>
> (vv. 154-65)

Rather than having a vision of a child who will redeem mankind by his self-chosen death on the tree of the cross, Zeborea dreams

---

[7] Edited by Carl Allen Tyre, "Religious Plays of 1590," *University of Iowa Studies in Spanish Literature* 8 (1938): 71-112.

that her son will be a traitor who also will die a self-chosen death. But it will be a suicide on a tree of iniquity inspired by the devil in conformity with the election of sin which Judas will make. The details of the woman's vision are calculated to establish at the outset of the work the poet's reliance on a conception of Judas as man the anti-Christ.

Faithful to the Renaissance decorative and allegorical demands of dramatic art, the anonymous author reinforces his presentation of Judas *praeparto* with a farcical interlude involving Lucifer's commission to Enbidia as a sort of "anti-guardian angel" of the child. Enbidia is, of course, an appropriate choice. The presence and influence of envy personified as the guardian of Judas's predetermined Cain role will explain and justify the forces of sin and evil, with Judas as their human embodiment (just as the forces of good and grace are embodied in the betrayal of Christ). Observe the fact that Lucifer is made to acknowledge the prescriptions of heaven as a source of the drama which Judas is about to become caught up in:

> *Luçifer.*   Pues, consuelo,
> rresta mudar el vestido
> y seguir al que es naçido;
> verás lo que hordena el çielo.
> *Enbidia.*   ¿Estoy bien?
> *Luçifer.*   Enbidia, sí.
> *Enbidia.*   ¿Cómo se llama?, y no más.
> *Luçifer.*   Judas, por siempre jamás
> y con esto yrás de aquí.
>   Aora, por ser tan pequeño,
> bástale Enbidia al donzel.
> *Enbidia.*   Yo daré tal quenta d'él
> que nos salga çierto el sueño.
> *Luçifer.*   Pues be en paz, hija querida.
> *Enbidia.*   Poca paz podrá yr conmigo,
> mas lo será paz, te digo,
> de te prosperar la vida.
>
>   (vv. 194-209)

The poet's presentation of Simon and Zeborea's dilemma is a frank accommodation of the circumstances of the holy family: both must grapple with the quandry of a child obviously singled out by destiny for a role which will mark him as different and which will continually bewilder his family. The solution reached by Judas's parents, however, represents a major parting of the ways between the two types. Following a well-established legend, Simon, rather than sheltering his son as Joseph will protect Jesus, decides to abandon the child to nature. As Simon leaves the child, Enbidia appears to articulate the major figural preoccupation of the *Comedia* that the divine plan has assigned to Judas a unique and vital role in its execution:

> Sentençia dabâ el donzel,
> mas, ¿he de matarle yo?
> Mátele el que le crió,
> que no tengo parte en él.
> Mi Judas, perded cuydado
> que de aquesta vez muráis,
> porque sabe Dios que estáis
> para mayor mal guardado.
> Sólamente os pondré aquí
> y si os tiene en quenta Dios,
> Dios hará por mí y por vos,
> y por vos solo sin mí.
> La provinçia es apartada
> de Jerusalém gran trecho;
> rresta sosegar mi pecho
> de más pecho quêstá armada.
> Si aqueste lugar conbiene
> a la hordenaçión del çielo,
> aquí topará el mozuelo
> aqueste tropel que viene.
>
> (vv. 266-85)

This preoccupation of the poet with the fact that heaven, not hell, has disposed Judas's role in the events of history, is of great importance in the conceptual unity of the work. Like a good and orthodox Christian, the author avoids the frequent temptations of the heresies which we popularly—if somewhat inaccurately—call Manichean. These heresies held that the universe witnesses a constant tension between a God of good and a God of evil, with both representing autonomous and powerful forces. Christianity attempted to repress this "heresy," which has had an enormous popularity in western culture (Saint Augustine, one recalls, was such a heretic before his conversion), insisting instead that evil was only the absence of grace and the reflex of the fall, and that, when God's plan would be realized ultimately in the Last Judgment, evil would forever be banished.

Thus, in a certain and logical sense, evil is a necessary ingredient in the contemporary world, for it is an important catalyst in the working out and resolution of divine history. For this reason, we may say that in a very simplistic sense Adam-Cain is vitally important for giving meaning and justification to Adam-Abel as he is incarnated as Christ. In this context we interpret and assign importance to Enbidia's comment at this point in the play's development.

The poet now turns the attention of his audience to Judas's adoption by Elisa and the dramatization of the first prefigurement of Judas's final betrayal. Legend has it that Elisa discovers the child —in some versions he is discovered floating in the waters (the comparison with Moses, a prefigurement of Christ, is obvious). In this text, Judas is discovered by the queen on the plain where he had been abandoned by his father. Elisa's reaction is ecstatic: "¡O figura divina y verdadera!" (v. 301), words which, in the context of the legend, can only be understood with an ironically superior point of view by the audience. Enbidia, who is with the child when he is discovered, tells the queen of Judas's origin, attributing to the parents an unconscious reference to their son as their likeness— the anti-Christ who is the image of the original sin of mankind: " 'Quedad con Dios, mi Judas y mi espexo ...' " (v. 313). The first *jornada* concludes with Judas's adoption by Elisa in place of the natural son which she has been denied. Given the events which follow, it is entirely justifiable to see the woman's closing words as charged with an unconscious irony, not only for the way in which Judas is going to betray his adoptive mother, but more significantly the way in which he is going to belie with his sins against mankind the words of divine litany which she applies to him:

> Con esto nos entremos, mi heredero,
> mi Judas, mi señor, mi luz y abrigo;
> sabrá el rrey lo que pasa y lo que quiero
> y gozará tanbién de oy más conmigo.
>
> (vv. 334-37)

The *jornada segunda* (vv. 338-680) opens with the king's soliloquy of doubt as to his wife's wisdom, as he wishes that "solo Dios quês bueno / nos libre del poder del hijo ageno" (v. 353). The adoptive father's intuitions became vivid reality as a chain of events begins which justify his disquiet: an attempted rape of the servant girls and violent fights with the king's men.

This segment of the play has been criticized for jumbled structure. [8] The apparent confusion begins with these words by the king:

> Ya la rreyna está preñada
> y en pariendo, yo os señalo
> que a de ber el hombre malo
> su pribanza bien trocada.
> Priba como no ay más d'el;
> mas como nazca el que aguardo
> yo os doy nuebas del bastardo
> que a de bolar de tropel.
>
> (vv. 374-81)

There then follows a short scene concerning Judas's fight with the king's men. The king assures them that they need not worry, for the queen has just given birth to a son who will replace the intruder. Verses 401-73 are a vignette in which Christ consoles the Virgin just before his passion. That Christ's role has been preordained and that his mission has been foretold by the prophets is made quite clear by the dialogue in this interlude. [9]

While one might argue that the juxtaposition here is dramatically clumsy, the author's purpose is clear. Judas is the intruder, the usurper, the "hijo ageno." Although in the inmediate context of Elisa, it is her own son who will drive Judas out, the inserted vignette makes it obvious that the true "hijo legítimo" is Christ himself, whose birth is to free mankind from the dreadful threat of the Judas-Cain. That the poet wishes us to see Elisa's son as a prefigurement of Jesus in his relationship with Judas has been advanced by the king's previous words. The most telling proof, however, comes in the following segment where Judas and his servant (Enbidia in disguise) plot to kill Elisa's real son, Tindoro. The latter senses Judas's intent and charges him with the stigma of the damned:

> Pues, cuytado, ¿en qué pequé
> yo en nazer?, triste de vos.

---

[8] Tyre in his introduction, p. 19.

[9] Compare the words of Mary, the *Mater dolorosa* in vv. 146-49. Notice the similarity in verse numbers; one is tempted to make an issue of the sacramental number 300 which separates these two speeches.

Quexaos sólamente a Dios
que sola la causa fué.
¿Cómo, si Dios fué seruido
de que yo naçiese aquí,
tiene de purgarse en mí
la culpa de aber naçido?
(vv. 533-40)

Using the familiar topos of the "no haber nacido," the poet invests Tindoro's speech with obvious irony. [10] Tindoro's words are to no avail, and Judas kills his "brother" while answering his accusations with words which are also ironic in the implication of their play on the words *trayçión* and *traydor*:

¿Mi pena os causa dolor?
Si hésa es trayçión o buen zelo,
yréis a dar quenta al çielo,
y aquí moriréis, traydor.
(vv. 565-68)

Judas has now fully revealed his nature and prefigured his final role in the Lord's design. In establishing the Cain/Abel, anti-Christ/Christ relationship between Judas and Tindoro, the poet has set up the polarities for the eventual working out of the "mayor mal" for which Judas is intended.

The second *jornada* concludes with an altercation of governing rights between Herodes and Pilatos, both of course anti-Christ temporal kings whose contest for power is ironically irrelevant in view of the Coming of Christ. Judas takes refuge from his crime in the service of Pilatos.

In the *jornada tercera* (vv. 681-1012), the poet pursues his legendary sources, and, just as the dramatic culmination of the second act was Judas's typical murder of his "brother," the third act centers around events leading up to Judas's unknowing assassination of his father over some fruit which he steals for Pilatos from Simon's garden (the fruit is, of course, *manzanas*).

The *jornada* begins with Lucifer ordering Yra to replace Enbidia as Judas's "guardian angel" (vv. 693-700). Thus, the anonymous

---

[10] See Alberto Porqueras Mayo, "Más sobre Calderón: 'Pues el delito mayor del hombre es haber nacido'; contribución al estudio de un 'topos' literario en España," *Segismundo* 2 (1965): 275-99.

dramatist refines the symmetry of the two central acts of his work. Both show Judas in important contexts—the court of the king and Pilatos's household—and both show him guided unknowingly by personifications of vices which are to channel him in the fulfillment of his role. It is a role whose ultimate denouement in *jornada cuarta* is prefigured in the murder, significantly, of first his "brother" (a Christ figure) and then his father, thereby defying the two people to whom he owes responsibility as a man. The climax comes when Yra praises Judas on his action and recommends to him Pilatos's protection, a "false *árbol*" which stands in a figural relationship to the tree of Eden and the fall of man, the apple tree which has caused Simon's death, and the true tree of the cross:

> Vn hecho as hecho, escojido,
> digno que por tal se diga.
> Agora te aparta y aguija,
> cuenta a Pilatos tu grima,
> quêl que a buen árbol se arrima
> buena sombra le cobija.
>
> (vv. 791-96)

This entire segment is underscored by the heavy irony characteristic of the work. Immediately prior to his death, Simon and his wife are discussing in the mellowness of their years the son whom they abandoned. Following her husband's death, Zeborea laments her widowhood, which, again according to the legend, Pilatos remedies by having Judas marry his own mother, still unrecognized. The dramatic profit to be derived from including this indignity to conventional morality is important in rounding out the personality which Judas has developed in the course of the play. That it is an unconscious sin is of little concern, since Judas's whole destiny is emphasized as being one assigned to him for the fulfillment of history. Thus Judas is unaware of the legions of evil, Enbidia and Yra, which guide him. The only suggestion of personal guilt is to be found in Yra's (ironic?) use of *escojido* in verse 791, quoted above.

The *jornada quarta* (vv. 1013-1408) completes the figural pattern which our *Comedia* has been underlining in its symmetrical presentation of the events of prefigurement leading up to Judas's final, infamous betrayal. As the legend has it, Judas and his mother finally

recognize each other. [11] Judas's reaction suggests that he has become
aware of his Cain stigma and the truth of Tindoro's observations:

> ¡O caso que no se a oýdo!
> ¡O hijo tal como yo,
> hijo que al padre mató!
> ¡Otro que yo no es naçido!
>
> (vv. 1101-04)

> ¡Desventurado y perdido
> hombre de ynfeliz manera,
> hombre tal que mereçiera
> la vida no aber naçido!
> ¿Adónde yrás?, sin ventura,
> lleno de culpas mortales,
> pues no me muestran los males
> parte que sea sigura.
> ¡Ay, tal pena para mi!
>
> (vv. 1125-33)

Zeborea suggests to him that he seek forgiveness of his sins by
joining the man Jesus, whose preachings offer the promise of salvation. The stage is now set for the precipitous fulfillment of Judas's
part in history. Christ accepts Judas as an apostle in words charged
with an irony which only time can make clear. Hesitating a moment,
Jesus goes on to say:

> ¿A qué veniste, cuytado?
> ¿A qué veniste, mezquino?
> ¿Quién te puso en el camino
> de tu muerte y triste estado?
> ¿A qué veniste, perdido?
> ¿A ver el mal que se espera?
> Dixeras: "Mejor me fuera
> ni venir ni aber naçido."
> Amigo, quiero admitirte
> pues lloras el mal pasado.
>
> (vv. 1213-22)

---

[11] It is interesting to note that in these lines, the poet includes the suggestion of a reason for Judas's unwholesome fate. Echoing the words of the
mother of the *Reyes d'Orient* (see the discussions in first part of this chapter),
Zeborea, perhaps as a figure of Eve, admits that her son possibly "Nacio
por mal de su madre" (v. 1065).

In order for Judas's part to attain completion, we must see him fulfill the prefigurements of acts 2 and 3. In act 4, the malefactor is finally in the company of the Son of Man, and the last impetus must be given to his true and preordained nature. Thus, Lucifer sends forth the third "guardian angel" in the form of the personified vice, Codiçia:

> ¡O Codiçia en quien se ençierra
> el bien quên mi rreyno mora!
> ¡Quien te biese ser señora
> del ynfiel quêstá en la tierra!
> Siempre alcanzaste victoria,
> Codiçia, mas ya el sentido
> que ninguno se a ofreçido
> que te diese tanta gloria.
> ¡O Codiçia! ¡No seas fría;
> éntrate y ponle calor;
> no se te baya el traydor;
> tócale, quêl alma es mía!
>
> (vv. 1285-96)

In each of the preceding acts Judas's one figural role has been crystallized in a series of immediate acts inspired by the vices of man: Envy has caused him to kill Tindoro; Anger, to assassinate his father; and, finally, Greed will lead him to betray the Savior. It is interesting and important to observe that Judas's final betrayal is not portrayed in direct, dramatic action on the stage. Rather, the poet chooses to refer to it indirectly through the confrontation between Lucifer and Judas, the latter condemned to hell for his betrayal and subsequent suicide.

The reason behind such a choice lies most likely in the author's desire not to portray the story of Christ, who figures only marginally in the work, but rather to underscore emphatically the life of Judas and his role as a figure of Adam-Cain, the sinner, the condemned, and the betrayer in original sin of mankind. Thus, the *Comedia* concludes with the juxtaposition of Judas the anti-Christ and Lucifer the anti-Lord. Judas's tears over his betrayal are in vain. Deprived of his support by the guiding vices and confronted finally by the terrible vision of what he has wrought for himself and for all mankind, he can only cringe with the audience at Lucifer's closing cry:

Yo me boy pues ya he dado
fin a lo que pretendía;
ya salí con mi porfía,
y el miserable, burlado.
Esto tengo por ofiçio
después que caý del çielo,
ocuparme acá en el suelo
en semejante exerçiçio.

(vv. 1401-08)

Lucifer, as he is presented in this play, comes to correlate with Adam-Cain as the incarnation of the power of the sinner, a power which has finally come to incarnate itself in the figure of the hapless Judas. In choosing to elaborate the function of Judas in divine history, our poet does not relate the story of man's redemption— although there is little doubt in the mind of the audience that Lucifer's words are a vain boast. Instead, the far-reaching consequences of the fall from grace are the central concern here, and we can only appreciate the intricate and symmetrical structure of the *Comedia* by acknowledging its insistence on detailing the life of Judas as the most frighteningly powerful figure of the stigma of Adam-Cain upon mankind.

Segund diz' Jhesuxristo, non ay cosa escondida,
Que a cabo de tienpo non sea bien sabida.

(s. 90)

If one were to seek a consensus among Juan Ruiz scholars it would be to find that the *Libro de buen amor* has consistently refused to yield itself to an interpretation, either partial or total, satisfactory to all interested parties. Indeed, it would seem that many scholars have spent as much time in denying the validity of each other's views as they have in applying themselves to the study of what is perhaps the most complex and perplexing work of medieval Spanish literature. [12] Some of the most illustrious names of Spanish scholarship have been involved in a debate which is still very much alive today as to precisely how the author would have us understand his

---

[12] The passion and intensity with which scholars have thrown themselves into the debate over the problems of interpretation are brought out in R. M. de Hornedo, "Pasión en torno a la crítica del Arcipreste," *Razón y fe* 162 (1961): 607-22.

poem. There are those who fervently affirm its straightforward autobiographical nature, whereby Juan Ruiz is speaking solely in terms
of Juan Ruiz. [13] These critics are opposed by their colleagues who
have a didactic-allegorical intent for the poem, whereby the "I" of
the poem is a rhetorical device to be taken as all mankind. [14] An
uneasy compromise is reached in the theories that the *Libro de buen
amor* has direct Arabic or Jewish antecedents which are both auto-

---

[13] In addition to the Hornedo article, the following studies contain extensive evaluations of the standing criticism on the *Libro de buen amor*:
A. Benito Durán, *Filosofía del Arcipreste de Hita. Sentido filosófico del
"Libro de buen amor"* (Alcoy, 1946); María Rosa Lida de Malkiel, "Nuevas
notas para la interpretación del "Libro de buen amor," *Nueva revista de
filología hispánica* 13 (1959): 17-82; Jorge Guzmán, *Una constante didáctico-
moral del Libro de buen amor* (Mexico, 1963). Given these four studies, it
would be superfluous for me to mention all of the critics who have supported this or that point of view. Therefore, I have limited myself to as few
references as possible. Concerning the autobiographical approach to Juan
Ruiz, the most recent work is Claudio Sánchez-Albórnoz, *España, un enigma
histórico* (Buenos Aires, 1957), 451-533. In his "Originalidad creadora del
Arcipreste," *Cuadernos del Congreso por la libertad de la cultura* 47 (1961):
75-83, Sánchez-Albórnoz reaffirms his position while artfully attacking Mrs.
Malkiel's opinions in her "Nuevas notas."

[14] A. Benito Durán, and Thomas R. Hart, *La alegoría en el Libro de
buen amor* (Madrid, 1959), are prominent examples of this group. See also
Leo Spitzer, "Note on the Poetic and the Empirical 'I' in Medieval Authors,"
Traditio 4 (1946): 414-22, who writes: "I would suggest that the Archpriest,
in using this self-incriminating procedure, wished to depict the potential
sinner which existed in himself, as in all human beings; he reveals himself,
not as having committed the sins he describes, but as capable, in his human
weakness, of having committed them" (p. 419). G. B. Gybbon-Monypenny,
"Autobiography in the *Libro de buen amor* in the Light of Some Literary
Comparisons," *Bulletin of Hispanic Studies* 34 (1957): 63, 78, demonstrates
that there is a long tradition of medieval autobiographical literature in which
the "I" can be either literal or allegorical-didactic. I might add that many
of them also might be figural, along the lines of my following discussions.
Although Gybbon-Monypenny does not mention the figural, he contributes
one very important observation in keeping with the tradition when he suggests
that "In seeking to explain the form of the *Libro de buen amor* we should
be thinking in terms, not of autobiography, but of the use of the first person
as a narrative technique" (p. 65). My point is that the figural relies on the
latter device for a very good reason, but in no way is the very literal
personality of Juan Ruiz to be denied either. Many of the critical controversies are due to the inability of some medievalists to accord Ruiz a freedom
of creativity which we accord as a matter of course to more recent writers.
Those critics who go to the other extreme and affirm that he is Spain's "first
modern poet" are merely reacting to the straitjacket imposed by unimagina-
tive philologists who would have the medieval poets as confined as possible
to a few easily recognizable models.

biographical and didactic at the same time.[15] All of these critical investigations are characterized by one obvious factor: they have attempted to put forth an absolute interpretation of the *Libro de buen amor* based on an analysis from the point of view of the history of ideas and literary tradition.

However, recent criticism has seen the introduction of another, possibly more fruitful, orientation. Anthony N. Zahareas in his recent study approaches this enigmatic work from the point of view of an artistic creation which is preoccupied first and foremost with achieving an aesthetic effect.[16] Shunning at first any attempt to offer a unified interpretation of the work, Zahareas examines painstakingly and in detail each of the major facets of the work. His sustaining interest is in revealing what he believes to be the archpriest's artistic self-consciousness, a concern which leads Ruiz to avoid simplistic, didactic interpretations of man and of his nature and to dwell upon our very real and painful moral ambivalency toward "buen" and "loco amor" in the face of our glaring human weaknesses. Thus, Zahareas is able to demonstrate—successfully I feel—that the *Libro de buen amor* is basically a work of art which gains its greatest inspiration from the poet's acute awareness that man is neither bad nor good, but simply human. It is an awareness which enables him to mold and to transform his sources along the lines of a more indulgent and understanding comprehension of man's failing than would be possible if the poet were concerned only with accepting or rejecting Christian virtue.

Although Zahareas does not so state, it is obvious that he has been influenced in his study by the tenets of New Criticism, particularly those which hold that one of the major characteristics of great art is its ambiguous nature deriving from the artist's ability to see mankind and human nature in more than just the black and white of the moral doctrinaire. The critic examines the fluctuating

---

[15] Américo Castro, *La realidad histórica de España* (Madrid, 1954), ch. 12, maintains the influence of the Spanish-Arabic *mudéjar* literature. Mrs. Malkiel, "Nuevas notas," while attacking Castro's position, advances her own theories of the influence of the Spanish-Jewish *maqamat*. Her ideas have been condensed in *Two Spanish Masterpieces: The Book of Good Love and The Celestina* (Urbana, Ill., 1961), pp. 18-33.

[16] Anthony N. Zahareas, *The Art of Juan Ruiz, Archpriest of Hita* (Madrid, 1965). Chapter 1 also contains an excellent summary of standing criticism.

meanings of the moral tags used in the poem in the light of his basic asumption that Ruiz subjugates these tags to his artistic interest in man's moral dilemma. Insisting on the structure of irony essential to the work, an irony which has led other critics to a defense of the prominence of loco amor, the critic is able to underline the ways in which the poet adds depth to his tales by forcing our understanding of the irony of man's position in Christian morals.

After extensively analyzing the structure and the rhetoric of the work, Zahareas ventures the following conclusion:

> The two fundamental issues in the critical assessment of Juan Ruiz have been, first, whether the *Libro de buen amor* is merely a miscellany presented through the conventional device of literary autobiography or an integrated work which might properly be said to have a theme; second, whether the theme of the *Libro* is religious or secular. As with all such questions, it is impossible to exclude entirely either possibility. However, the nature of the problem itself, the "either-or" possibility points to a central fact about the *Libro* whether it reveals a theme or not. For in order to formulate a hypothesis about the theme or pervading spirit of the *Libro,* it is necessary to take into account both the narrator's enthusiasm about secular love and his inclusion of comments and stories decidedly Christian in spirit. We cannot, however, penetrate the *Libro*'s complexity if we slight the Archpriest's wordly preoccupations to study principally the didactic orientation, nor if we overlook completely the moral teachings to point out the secular preoccupations. We must, rather, account for both of them and, above all, not misinterpret the *Libro* by reading into it patterns which may belong to its sources but which we do not actually find in it. ...
>
> Although set in a didactic framework, the *Libro* is, nevertheless, an elaborate scrutiny of the conflict between realistic human values and the abstract code of divine love. ... Under the pressures of this everyday world, the *raison d'être* of *buen amor,* at first seemingly unquestionable, begins to crumble. ... The one definite blow to the arguments viewing the *Libro* as a manual of *buen amor,* and thus to the whole didactic structure, comes when the Archpriest, given his choice as the narrative's commentator, chooses not to choose definitely at all. However much Juan Ruiz finds *buen amor* a spiritual consolation, he remains hesitant to desert the idea of cupidity with all its pleasure and joys. (pp. 202-03)

Zahareas thus opens a whole new range of possibilities for studying Juan Ruiz's complex artistic procedure. He examines many of them himself, always bearing in mind that what he analyzes contributes to our understanding of the *Libro de buen amor* as essentially a human document and only in parts, and then most definitely in an ironic sense, a didactic treatise.

One of the topics which concerns Zahareas's examination of the archpriest's artistry is the role which allegory plays in the structure of the work. Although he rightly evaluates many of the supposedly allegorical passages as more appropriately examples of the poet's all-pervading irony, there are nevertheless many segments of the work which employ a form of allegory as a means for portraying the moral ambivalence of the human soul in the face of Christian ideals and its own earthy nature. The following discussion will respect Zahareas's general conclusions regarding the *Libro de buen amor* while advancing the figural interpretation as one of the devices of which the poet avails himself in describing the moral ambivalence of man, now Adam the saint, now Adam the sinner. [17]

The *Libro de buen amor* may be divided into the following principal parts: [18]

stanzas 1-10	opening prayer
prose prologue	
stanzas 11-43	prayer and Gozos de Santa María
stanzas 44-70	"disputación de los griegos é los romanos"
71-76	Aristotle's "principle"
77-180	Early love experiences, including the vanities of the world, Fernand García and the importance of the Constellations
stanzas 181-891	Doña Endrina affair, beginning with dispute with Don Amor, advice from Doña Venus, imitation of Pamphilus's *De amore*, ending with the marriage of Don Melón and Doña

[17] Hart discusses allegory in his study. However, as María Rosa Lida de Malkiel, in her review in *Romance Philology* 14 (May, 1961): 342, points out, Hart is too intent on seeing allegory where the poet, contrary to supposed medieval poetic practice, has failed to announce its presence. Hart's work is also devoted to a panallegorical interpretation of the *Libro*, an interpretation which Zahareas's structural studies, especially those dealing with the roles of narrator and participant, seem to render highly doubtful. In addition, Hart's study of the *Libro de buen amor* is far weaker in its organization and arguments than his previously cited papers on the "Conde Arnlados" and *Sibila Cassandra*.

[18] All quotations from the *Libro de buen amor* in this study are according to J. Cejador y Frauca's edition (Madrid, 1963).

	Endrina. Stanzas 217-316 are examples of how *loco amor* leads to the seven deadly sins
892-909	advice to ladies on the moral of the Endrina episode
stanzas 910-1042	other love experiences, including the *serranas*
stanzas 1043-66	prayers and passion of Our Lord
1067-1314	battle beteen Don Carnal and Doña Quaresma, ending in the triumph of Don Carnal
stanzas 1315-1519	Doña Garoça and "La mora" affairs
1520-78	death of Trotaconventos
1579-1605	Armas del Xristiano
stanzas 1606-25	encomium on "dueñas chicas" and the description of Don Ffurón
stanzas 1626-1709	epilogue material, containing further clarification of *buen amor,* Gozos de Santa María, prayer of the "scolares," various prayers to the Virgin, concluding with the "cántica de los clérigos"

The most salient characteristic of this summary is the extensive space given over to the colloquies with Don Amor and Doña Venus, the Endrina affair, the *serranas,* and the battle between Don Carnal and Doña Quaresma. In other words, much space is devoted to loco amor. [19] Most critics, no matter what their interpretation of

---

[19] Benito Durán attributes the predominance of "loco amor" to the very nature of the work: "Para el Arcipreste de Hita el problema de su propia propensión a amar "dueñas de buen linaje e de mucha nobleza" le llevó a formular un determinismo erótico en el hombre, muy difícil o casi imposible de vencer, sino es por un milagro de Dios. He ahí la clave con que se ha de interpretar o descifrar el *Libro de buen amor,* según nosotros entendemos. Ve, desde luego, una ley natural tan fatal como universal, en el amor, considerado como afán "por aver juntamiento con fembra placentera" (p. 55). In his own opinion, Durán is supported by Zahareas's valuable conclusion that Ruiz is concerned first and foremost with the nature of man. Concerning the nature of Ruiz's ambivalent Prologue, see Pierre Liullman, "Juan Ruiz's Prologue," *Modern Language Notes* 82 (1967):149-70.

buen amor may be, [20] appear to agree that loco amor is equivalent to sin, and thus have concluded that, despite the prologue and the opening and closing praises to the Virgin, Juan Ruiz's poem must be seen as an "ars amandi" and as a defense of sexual love. [21] The argument, supposedly founded on impeccable common sense, is that if loco amor equals sin and sexual love, and if such is the main interest of the poem, then the poem must be pro sin and sexual love. Such an argument overlooks several significant points. To the extent that sin predominates in the world, a work dealing with the "pelea" between the "I" of the poem and Don Amor plausibly would dwell on the ways sin holds sway over men's souls. Mrs. Malkiel has spoken of how such is, in fact, a common procedure in medieval literature. [22] One need only recall the Corbacho, a book whose didactic intent is beyond dispute, but which is nevertheless a work replete with examples of loco amor. A second overlooked factor is the degree to which loco amor equals the sin of loco amor as it is taught by the pagan tradition—the old order of the universe—and the degree to which that tradition survives despite the option which man has for divine grace. Allegorical interpretation of the Libro de buen amor, in their decision to disavow truth or validity in the real and sincere involvement of the work's narrator with loco amor and in their corresponding desire to see sincerity in the only real intent of the poem (to be found in the pious Marian hymns affirming a love of grace), overlook the possibilities of seeing both sin and grace as living, struggling, and surviving side by side, and the further

---

[20] The various ideas on the subject are put forth in G. B. Gybbon-Monypenny, " 'Lo que buen amor dize con rrazon te lo pruebo,' " Bulletin of Hispanic Studies 38 (1961): 13-24.

[21] Cf. Felix Lecoy, Recherches sur le "Libro de buen amor" de Juan Ruiz, Arcipreste de Hita (Paris, 1938): À notre avis, l'hésitation n'est guère permise: le Libro de buen amor est un art d'aimer" (p. 360).

[22] Two Spanish Masterpieces: "The habit of presenting moral and religious teachings in a facetious way goes against the grain of the modern reader, but the medieval authors who advocate and practice this device are too numerous to be cited. ... The habit of making an abstract lesson palpable by means of a jocular story received support also from the allegorical exegesis of the scripture, obligatory in the Middle Ages for Jews, Christians and Muslims alike. ... Conversely, the writer felt authorized to compose stories totally devoid of austerity, and to point out later that, aside from the literal, purely entertaining meaning, the reader could detect other more valuable meanings, in harmony with his moral and intellectual capacity" (pp. 30-31).

possibility of the medieval poet's having portrayed the tension of this forced cohabitation. The survival of sin even after the Coming of Christ is the basic point of departure for the Bible and the subsequent writings of the church fathers. Sin—loco amor—was far from eradicated by the sacrifice of Christ. The final triumph of grace is yet to come with the fulfillment of the eschatological prophecies of the Bible. Thus, sin endures and man struggles with the reality of living in its constant presence. [23] It is in accord with this reality of medieval Christianity that we may begin to understand the hardy stamina of sin and loco amor in the *Libro de buen amor*. Juan Ruiz is not writing of the final judgment of mankind, when the problems of the soul will reach their ultimate resolution. He is writing of the struggle of man with sin and virtue when both vie for his attention, with the former being the most attractive. We have little reason to doubt the sincerity of the poem's narrator as he repeatedly orders Don Amor to be gone during their long encounter at the outset of the work. His ultimate yielding to Don Amor's promises does not make his protestations less sincere, but only reflects ironically—and hilariously—the flaw in human nature to which the sacrament of penance owes its existence. Man sins because he is man. This is an acknowledged reality in medieval Christianity at least.

In terms of figural intepretation, Juan Ruiz works out his portrayal of sin from the pagan tradition, the starting point for human history. Not only is it the source of man's fall and sinful nature, but it is the treasure house of the "immoral" works of the non-Christian poets whose high esteem the church fathers struggled so valiantly to usurp with their allegorical and figural interpretations. [24] We are familiar now with the degree to which they were

---

[23] Benito Durán: "Tal es a nuestro modo de ver el Poema de Buen Amor: obra de filosofía; de la filosofía de la vida real y concreta, cuando en ella el hombre se ve acuciado por el mayor de los problemas; el encadenamiento de su alma a la fuerza diabólica de la carne con la perspectiva de una eterna pérdida de aquélla y de su eterno valor. He ahí la ironía trágica del Poema" (p. 35).

[24] Henry Osborn Taylor, *The Classical Heritage of the Middle Ages* (New York, 1958) writes with respect to art that "The Christian authors had renounced the pagan religion, they condemned its idolatry, some of them disapproved pagan literature. But one and all were educated in standards of artistic taste and principles of literary composition which were the fruit of pagan culture. ... But these classic rules were profoundly irreconcilable with the spirit of the new Christian matter, as may be readily seen in Christian

unsuccessful in doing away with the pagan tradition. And we are equally familiar with the way in which they accomodated the older tradition, from the Old Testament to Ovid's *Ars amandi* to the Christian tradition. The figural interpretations of the Jewish Law by St. Paul in his epistles to the Corinthians and Dante's artful adjustment of the pagan poets to his Christian vision of the universe in the *Divina commedia* are the two most outstanding examples of one solution to a conflict which kept the Middle Ages alive with writers producing works such as the *Ovide moralisé* (early fourteenth-century).

With respect to Juan Ruiz, who deals with sin in terms of love and sex, it is therefore not surprising to find that Ovid, if not exercising a direct influence, has become the supreme authority for pagan love. [25] From the beginning of the archpriest's dispute with Don Amor to his escape from the lecherous clutches of the four *serranas*, the *Libro de buen amor* is dominated by the shadow of Ovid, by the tactics for the would-be medieval playboy attributed to him, and by the general atmosphere of a sinful world in which the sixth commandment does not rule. It is a domination of pagan and non-Christian love broken only by the marriage of Doña Endrina and Don Melón and the author's "advice to young ladies" on how the Endrina exemplum is to be taken.

If one considers the poem in terms of the progression of events leading up to the prayers which follow the episodes of the *serranas*,

---

poetry" (p. 7). Otis Green quotes E. Harris Harbison, *The Christian Scholar in the Age of Reformation* (Princeton, N. J., 1956): "Each lived on in his books—Jerome in his *Letters,* Augustine in his *Confessions,* Abelard in his *Sic et Non,* Aquinas in his *Summa Theologica*—and in each a question was embodied of the sort that must be answered anew by each succeeding generation of Christians...: Is it possible to synthesize Christianity and culture" (pp. 28-29).

[25] R. Schevill, *Ovid and the Renascence in Spain* (Berkeley, Calif., 1913), 28-54, "*El libro de buen amor,* by the Arcipreste de Hita and Its Indebtedness to Ovid." See also Edwin J. Webber, "Juan Ruiz and Ovid," *Romance Notes* 2 (1960): 54-57. In reality, the importance of whether or not Juan Ruiz was actually familiar with the texts of Ovid's writings diminishes when one realizes that insofar as Ovid by reputation during the Middle Ages is the supreme model for "love theory," Juan Ruiz and his contemporaries were familiar with his name and the ideas of his works, if not with the works themselves. Ovid is mentioned several times in the *Libro de buen amor,* particularly in the debate with Don Amor, who says: "Sy leyeres Ovyido, el que fué mi criado, / En él fallarás fablas, que l'ove yo mostrado" (s. 429).

the subtle working out of loco amor in terms of non-Christian, pagan morality becomes evident. Aside from the opening prologue and supporting prayers, the work begins with the "Disputación de los griegos é los romanos," which is not so much a starting point in pagan antiquity as it is an affirmation of the levels of meaning which the reader may find in any work and in this one in particular:

> En general á todos ffabla la escriptura:
> Los cuerdos con buen sesso entendrán la cordura,
> Los mançebos livianos guárdense de locura,
> Escoja lo mijor el de buena ventura.
> Las del Buen Amor sson razones encubiertas;
> Trabaja do fallares las sus señales çiertas;
> Ssi la rrazón entiendes ó en el sesso açiertas,
> Non dirás mal del libro, que agora rrehiertas.

> (ss. 67-68)

Such an affirmation, implied or expressly stated, is the accepted starting point for any medieval work purporting to be moral in nature. Following the "disputación" is the famous statement on natural love attributed to one of the most recognized of the pagan authorities, Aristotle:

> Como dize Aristóteles, cosa es verdadera:
> El mundo por dos cosas trabaja: la primera,
> Por aver mantenençia: la otra cosa era
> Por aver juntamiento con fenbra plazentera.

> (s. 71)

The illustrious Greek is followed by a parade of authorities who owe little to the Christian tradition: Ovid, astrology; [26] Don Amor

---

[26]   Yo creo los estrólogos verdad naturalmente;
> pero Dios, que crió natura é açidente,
> Puédelos demudar é fazer otramente,
> Segund la fe cathólica; yo desto so creyente.

> (s. 140)

The idea of the universe being ordered down to the last detail by God, who arranged history prophetically in accord with his plan, is a principle of medieval figural philosophy and of St. Thomas Aquinas's writings. See Chydenius, The Typological Problem in Dante ... (Helsinki, 1958), "The Senses of the Scripture According to St. Thomas Aquinas," pp. 38-41.

and Doña Venus; and most important of all, the exempla, the majority of which are taken from the non-Christian tradition. [27]

The use of exempla in support of both the pagan tradition and the Christian tradition is an excellent example of the medieval practice of the accommodation of texts, and points in turn to the strong relationship which exists between the non-Christian and the Christian traditions by virtue of the figural relationship between the two. The accommodation of texts refers not only to the practice of seeing the texts of the old order—antiquity and the Old Testament—in terms of their prefigurement of Christianity but also to the use of Christian texts in a sort of retrospective process whereby they are parodied in terms of values which their true meaning would reject. [28] There are several instances of this in Juan Ruiz's work, the best one of which is the parody of the canonical hours. [29] Another example of accommodated text in Juan Ruiz is the hymn in praise of Venus. Modeled on the Marian hymns, it underscores the figural relationship between Venus, the champion of pagan love, and Mary, the champion of Christian charity:

> "Señora doña Venus, muger de don Amor,
> "Noble dueña, omillome yo, vuestro servidor:
> "De todas cosas sodes vos é el Amor señor,
> "Todos vos obedesçen como á su fasedor.

> (s. 585)

In so artfully accommodating Christian texts to non-Christian values, the medieval poet is affirming the validity of the non-Christian values, although his parody itself is an acknowledgment of the "sinful" nature of his procedure. This lending support to a

---

[27] See the note on the exemplum tradition in Spain and its origins in John Esten Keller, *Motif-Index of Medieval Spanish Literature* (Knoxville, Tenn., 1949).

[28] Concerning accommodation of texts, see Charles Haskins, *The Renaissance of the Twelfth Century* (New York, 1957), pp. 183ff., where he quotes from the delightful "Evangelium secundum Marcos Argenti." In a more serious vein, see Ernst Robert Curtius, *European Literature and the Latin Middle Ages,* trans. Willard R. Trask (New York, 1953), Excursus VI, "Early Christian and Medieval Literary Studies," pp. 446-67.

[29] See Otis H. Green, "On Juan Ruiz's Parody of the Canonical Hours," *Hispanic Review* 26 (1958):12-34; included in a briefer form in his *Spain in the Western Tradition,* 1: 53-60.

claim of validity and reality for the older tradition is one of the primary distinctions between figural interpretation and allegory. In addition, it is in these passages where Juan Ruiz most succeeds as an artist in portraying the dilemma of all-too-earthly man.

Juan Ruiz initially portrays himself as struggling valiantly and heatedly against the overwhelming presence of Don Amor. The poet's equation of Don Amor's *loco amor* and sin is the cornerstone of a hypothesis concerning the figural implications of the *Libro de buen amor,* and it is an equation which the poet attempts to support by the long series of exempla marshaled to prove how *loco amor* occasions the seven deadly sins.

The sins mentioned are the sins of the old order inherited by Christianity:

> Contigo syenpre trahes los mortales pecados:
> Con la mucha cobdiçia, los omes engañados,
> Ffázesles cobdiçiar é ser muy denodados.
> Passar los mandamientos, que de Dios fueron dados.
>
> (s. 217)

It is noteworthy that all of the exempla and references are from or in terms of the non-Christian tradition. Nevertheless, Don Amor's arguments and promises are convincing, and the poet yields himself to the non-Christian master, Love. Love speaks about the poet's failures:

> Quesyste ser maestro ante que discípulo ser,
> E non sabes mi manera syn la de mí aprender;
> Oy' é leye mis castigos, é sabrás byen fazer ...
>
> (s. 427)

A high point of the section of the poem devoted to "hard-core sin" is the series of encounters with the *serranas* which, again, are quite real and credible in and of themselves, but which readily yield to a higher meaning on the basis of their mockery of courtly love, itself one resolution open to medieval man for the conflict between *loco amor* and *buen amor* and indeed the basis of the "happy ending" of the Doña Endrina affair. [30] From one point of view the

---

[30] Green, *Spain and the Western Tradition,* vol. 1, ch. 3, "Courtly Love," pp. 72-122, discusses the courtly love tradition and its relation to the sacra-

prayers following the poet's experiences with the *serranas* seem to be a violent and inexplicable juxtaposition of the crude and the devout. But such a juxtaposition occurs frequently in the Middle Ages and serves here to underline a basic Christian belief that the most despicable in man pleads no contest to the all-encompassing grace of God, provided only that a desire for grace is sincere. A problem arises, therefore, only if the critic undertakes to maintain the consistent insincerity of the poet in all passages indicating a recantation on his part.

What is more interesting is not the juxtaposition, but the content of what has been juxtaposed. If it is true that the episode of the *serranas* is Juan Ruiz's proof that loco amor and courtly love really lead to the same sin, [31] the prayers to Mary and the passion become highly significant at this point in the development of the work:

> Omíllome, Reyna,
> Madre del Salvador,
> Virgen Santa é dina,
> Oy' á mí, pecador.
> Mi alma en tí cuyda
> É en tu esperança:
> Virgen, tú me ayuda
> É syn toda tardança
> Rruega por mí á Dios, tu Fijo é mi Señor.
>
> (ss. 1046-47)

> En cruz fué por nos muerto,
> Ferido é llagado,
> E después fué abierto

---

ment of marriage. The principal basis of a resolution between the two is that the courtly love match is preordained by Fortune, and that, if the couple's love is pure and steady (even though they may fall into sin), the vows which they exchange in secret are as binding and as holy as those which they may exchange before a priest at a later time (p. 106). This arrangement was valid up to the Council of Trent and may explain why the "marriage" between Doña Endrina and Don Melón before Trota-conventos is presented as a valid resolution to the episode.

[31] See G. B. Gybbon-Monypenny, " 'Lo que buen amor dize con rrazon te lo pruebo.' " Although this critic rejects completely a "buen amor de Dios" in the *Libro,* his arguments in support of the buen amor of the courtly tradition as coming to equal loco amor for Juan Ruiz seem well founded.

D'ascona su costado:
Por estas llagas, çierto,
Es el mundo salvado.
Á los qu' en él creemos,
El nos quiera ssalvar.

(s. 1066)

In the next stanza the poet begins the long segment dealing
with the battle between Don Carnal and Doña Quaresma. Again, the
author's arrangement of his work is far from haphazard, and this
episode enjoys a particularly important artistic reason for its inclusion here. The passion of Christ, while bringing divine grace and
the possibility of salvation to mankind, does not automatically free
man from sin. The role of the Lenten season in Christianity is the
portrayal of man's constant struggle in the here and now between
the two choices open to him, represented by Doña Quaresma and
Don Carnal. Although the former is momentarily victorious, the
pageant of Easter is short-lived, and man, being man, soon lapses
back into his evil ways. The fact that the glory of the resurrection
is the occasion for the comically triumphant entrance of Don Amor
and the "resurrection" of the seven deadly sins attributed to him
underscores the essential irony for the poet of the Christian framework of the new order. The world continues to be plagued by sin,
and the renewal of Lent and Easter is a yearly ritual in which sin
is only temporarily suppressed. Don Amor's triumph is assured, and
the cycle begins all over again. Don Amor is a basic necessity, for
without the inevitable sinning of the sons of Adam the passion of
Christ in its daily reenactment in the sacrifice of the mass would
cease to have meaning and God's plan would have reached its
ultimate fulfillment.

Although Dante's poem reaches toward the meaning of God's
final design for the universe, Juan Ruiz's poem remains very
sardonically bound to the eternal sufferings of the "carne y hueso"
sinful man, attracted to grace, but inescapably wed to sin. [32] Indeed,

---

[32] Castro believes that the "in and out" Arabesque-like nature, the continual movement and activity of the work (p. 382), disqualifies it for didactic
literature: "El *Libro de buen amor* no cabe en los límites de la poesía
didáctica, en la cual la vida es contemplada fuera de ella, puesta entre
paréntesis y vista en la firme realidad del debe ser, no en la realidad de

I have attempted to show precisely this: that the texture of sin in the *Libro de buen amor* is basically pre-Christian and non-Christian, that Christianity, through the intercession of Mary, the Mediatrix and the way to grace, whom Trotaconventos and Venus may be said to prefigure in their temptation of man to sin, offers man the opportunity to escape from his sinful youth into the Church. Man's ambivalence and indecision in the face of this choice, a unique characteristic of Christianity explicated so well by Juan Ruiz's humorous stance as commentator and participant, far from being allegorical, is the very real history of the human race. That man's final choice will be for the divine grace of God's final judgment is the optimistic note on which the *Libro* ostensibly (but ironically?) concludes.

If one is willing to accept the possibility of Juan Ruiz's having made extensive use of the figural tradition, as I have presented it, for purposes of reinforcing his artistic intent to portray the reality of man's moral ambivalence, the subsequent episodes present little difficulty. There is the unsuccessful affair with Doña Garoça containing the several exempla presented by the go-between and her intended victim in support of their divergent points of view, the famous physical description of the archpriest, [33] and a brief palinode intended to demonstrate the didactic intent of this episode. [34] After describing a brief attempt at an affair with "una mora" and the accompanying non-Christian "canciones," often interpreted as

---

su existir" (p. 383). Whether or not the work is didactic is not really the point; rather, as I have tried to show, what is important is the relationship between sin and grace, the two poles between which the Christian oscillates in his day-to-day experience as both saint and sinner.

[33] A discussion of whether or not this description is of the archpriest must take into consideration the fact that Juan Ruiz was an old man when he wrote the *Libro*. Although he could easily be describing his younger self, see the position taken by Elisha Kent Kane, "The Personal Appearance of Juan Ruiz," *Modern Language Notes* 45 (1930):103-09, to the effect that enough topoi are used to make it a typical medieval physical description. I see no conflict in considering it both authentic and typical.

[34] Whether or not to believe that Juan calls Trotaconventos buen amor and names his poem after her (ss. 932-33), and whether or not Trotaconventos mentions "buen amor del amigo" (s. 1452) because such is the whole intent of the poem or because of circumstances in which irony, flattery, and courtly love are involved has been discussed at length by Guzmán, "Buen Amor," in *Una constante*, pp. 111-37.

showing Juan Ruiz's familiarity with the Jewish and Moorish communities, Trotaconventos dies, occasioning the poet's eulogy of the old bawd and his long invective at this juncture, again affirming the poet's interest in man's involvement with sin in relation to his possibilities for salvation. There is little reason to doubt the sincerity of the poet's words during this moment of "grief," for he has lost an extremely useful means for obtaining sinful pleasure. His is a lament not so much for the passing of sin as it is for one important occasion for it, a lament which moves toward a concluding consideration of the way in which man in his enthusiastic dedication to the "non" waits until he can no longer elude the beckoning hand of death before renouncing sin and switching his allegiance to the "sic":

> Allega el mesquino é non ssabe para quién:
> E maguer cada día esto así avién',
> Non has ome, que faga su testamento byen,
> Fasta que ya por ojo la muerte ve que vien'.
>
> (s. 1543)

Whether the modern reader considers this hypocritical or not becomes unimportant in view of the fact that this was and still is a common phenomenon, with the sinner absolutely sincere in his two opposing (and nonconcurrent) states of mind: "Sooner or later the 'delightful frenzy' of the world of men must be recognized for what it is, by every Christian. The world is ever with us, yet late or soon its enticements must be renounced. The believer moves through a maze of things forbidden, unmindful of the prohibitions, toward a repentance as inevitable as that of King David. In a culture as rigorous as the Spanish-Catholic, it is remarkable that, in all periods, the day of reckoning could be postponed and sin indulged in, often in a spirit of lightheartedness, though with full awareness that amends would of necessity be made, that the soul must certainly win in the struggle with the baser self. It was this, of course, that made literature possible" (p. 264). [35]

---

[35] Green, *Spain and the Western Tradition*, vol. 1, ch. 7, "Truancy and Recantation," pp. 264-99. See Frank P. Casa's study on the lament, "Toward an Understanding of the Arcipreste's Lament," *Romanische Forschungen* 73 (1967): 463-75.

Therefore, one should not be startled by the description of the "Armas del Xristiano" which follows the lament for Trotaconventos. The description of the seven deadly sins, paralleling the description of the sins occasioned by Don Amor (ss. 217-371), along with the sacraments and devices available to a Christian for defending himself from sin, is the appropriate palinode after the lament for Trotaconventos's demise. [36] I need not go into them here; suffice it to note that the sins brought about by love which are described earlier are not necessarily violations of a Christian code, while those sins following the passion which are described as defense measures against them are proposed in strictly Christian terms. They come up here in the poem to show how the "armas" may be used to combat them and to lead man to salvation:

> La carn', el diablo, el mundo; déstos nasçen los mortales,
> Déstos tres vienen los otros: tomemos armas atales,
> Que vençamos nos á ellos.
>
> (s. 1584)

Little more need be said concerning the concluding segments of the poem. Aside from problems of a textual nature, there is little outstanding. [37] The last 100 stanzas are devoted to a reaffirmation of the virtuous intent of the work and hinge on an added statement concerning buen amor:

> Pues este libro es de *Buen amor,* enprestadlo de grado:
> No l'negades su nonbre ni l' dedes rrheretado,
> No l' dedes por dinero vendido nin alquilado,
> Ca non ha grado nin graçia el *Buen amor* conplado.
>
> (s. 1630)

---

[36] Lecoy discusses the "armas" at length, showing the equivalencies established (pp. 184-85). Concerning the figural nature of the sacraments, see Jean Daniélou, *The Bible and Liturgy* (South Bend, Ind., 1956), which takes up the typology of the sacraments. Johan Chydenius, *The Theory of Medieval Symbolism* (Helsinki, 1960), is also useful on this subject.

[37] The reference here is to the position in the *Libro* enjoyed by "De las propiedades que las dueñas chicas han" (ss. 1606-17) and "De Don Ffurón moço del Arcipreste" (ss. 1618-25), a position which remains unexplained by any of the unified interpretations put forth. With regard to the two "Cantares de Ciego," according to Cejador y Frauca in his edition (2:286), they do not appear in the 1343 *S*-Ms, but are to be found in the 1330 *G*-Ms.

Whether Juan Ruiz supports in the final analysis buen amor or loco amor remains to a large extent a matter of personal interpretation and the acceptance of the many competent cases offered by a large body of widely divergent opinion. Nevertheless, on the level of artistic structure it is possible to see with respect to the virtues and vices of love that in elaborating his ever-changing approach to the reality of human experience, first as a man and second as an artist, Juan Ruiz is informed by the Christian figural concept of Adam's nature, which enables him to augment his vivid portrayal of the basically ironic and ambivalent nature of man and his behavior in "moral" situations with a traditional Christian concept of the everyday reality of the contest between the origins of the fall of man and the promises of his redemption. As in the case of Mary of Egypt, Juan Ruiz portrays sin to a large extent in a non-Christian or pre-Christian context. However, it is remarkably indicative of the sophistication of the later work that, rather than seeking a facile new-order resolution of sinful conflict, the *Libro de buen amor* reverberates with man's awareness of the essential tension which underlies the confrontation of the not-always-accepted ideal of Christian grace and inviting worldly sin. [38]

---

[38] Robert Walker's "Towards an Interpretation of the *Libro de buen amor*," *Bulletin of Hispanic Studies* 43 (1966):1-10, stresses the trajectory of the poem from a spirit of abandon to one emphasizing the sinfulness and stupidity of love and the triumph of death over all. Walker's observations lend a strong support to seeing a clean line of progression from happy sin to a grace tempered by fourteenth-century morbidity. Note the critic's sensitivity to Ruiz's complex moral ambivalence: "It is not necessary to argue that the Archpriest must come down on one side or the other, as most critics have done: surely it is possible for a man to have strong carnal leanings and at the same time a real faith in God and a sense of sin" (p. 4).

CHAPTER III

THE CONCEPT OF MARY IN THIRTEENTH-CENTURY
SPANISH POETRY

IN ONE OF THE MOST DELIGHTFUL OF ALFONSO'S *Cantigas*,[1] the poet employs a paronomasia to underline his concept of the role of the Virgin Mary in the history of mankind:[2]

> *Entre Ave Eva*
> *gran departiment'á.*
> Ca Eva nos tolleu
> o Parays' e Deus
> Ave nos y meteu;
> porend', amigos meus
> *entre Ave Eva*
> *gran departiment'á.*
> Eva nos foi deitar
> do dem' en sa prijon,

---

[1] *Antología de Alfonso X El Sabio*, ed. de Antonio G. Solalinde, 3ª ed. (Buenos Aires, 1946), p. 33. See also Cantigas 270 and 320 on the same theme. Texts found in *Cantigas de Santa María* (Madrid, 1889), 2:377 and 2:445 respectively.

[2] A similar paronomasia is to be found at the end of the first *auto* in Florence Whyte, "Three *Autos* of Jorge de Montemayor," *PMLA* 43 (1928): 953-89. As a device reminiscent of the etymological tradition exemplified by Isidore, the "ave/eva" comparison is "explained" in Spanish poetry in the fourteenth-century *Libro de miseria de homne* in a long segment beginning with stanza 42. See the edition by Manuel Artigas, "Un nuevo poema por la cuaderna vía ...," *Boletín de la Biblioteca Menéndez Pelayo*, 1 (1919): 31-37, 87-95, 153-61, 210-16, 328-38; 2 (1920): 41-48, 91-98, 233-54. The poem is a rhymed gloss on Innocent's *De contemptu mundi*, one of the most widely read medieval Latin compositions.

et Ave én sacar;
et por esta razón,
entre Ave Eva
gran departiment'á.
Eva nos fez perder
amor de Deus e ben,
e pois Ave aver
nol-o fez; o porén,
entre Ave Eva
gran departiment'á.
Eva nos enserrou
os çöes sen chave,
e María britou
as portas per Ave.
Entre Ave Eva
gran departiment'á.

The poet's paronomasia stresses the fact that there is more than a casual relationship between Eve and Mary. The elaboration of the contrast between the two is not particularly complex and relies heavily on some of the most common devotional topoi of the Middle Ages. A bimembration is established by the *estribillo* between the two figural aspects of woman—the temptress and the redemptress. In this case, the man is Everyman, and the scope of the poem is the history of mankind. The *Cantiga* pursues this basic bimembration throughout each of the four stanzas, with the first two lines of the *mudanza* referring to Eva's impact on mankind and the concluding verse to Ave's revision of the situation. The *estribillo* follows each stanza to insist upon the different roles of the two men.

The four stanzas discuss, respectively, the loss and recovery of paradise, the imprisonment of man and his subsequent freedom (cf. the "cárcel de amor" topos—an excellent example of Alfonso's treatment "a lo divino" of the commonplaces of love in his praises of the Virgin), man's lapse into indifference toward God and his change of feeling, and, finally (returning to the topic of the opening stanza), the sealing of heaven against man and the destruction of that seal. Although Alfonso's *Cantiga* reiterates what separates the two through the bimembrational treatment of the subject in each stanza, the final implication is that while the chasm is as deep between the two women as that which separates sin and grace, together they stand as the signpost for the grand sweep of the history of mankind.

Alfonso's poem appeals to the common belief of his audience that Mary's role as a prototype of feminine virtue was in some way foreshadowed and demanded by Eve, who throughout history has stood for the damnation of man by a woman.

It is necessary to make a distinction between the formal figural exegesis performed by church scholars with a restraint and a perspective grounded in theological studies, and the more casual and enthusiastic figural analogizing carried out by poets whose interests lay less in theology than in elaborating an artistic artifice. One of the principal ways in which the poets differed from the professional exegetes was in their conception of Mary as rivaling Christ in importance for the salvation of mankind. Although Alfonso is usually less audacious than others, there can be little doubt that as a poet he is more fascinated by the story of Mary, legendary and biblical, than he is by that of her son. His *Cantigas* attest to this fact, and the poem discussed above is generous in its evaluation of Mary's importance to mankind. In the analyses which follow, I attempt to show how, for other poets, Mary tends to be confused with Christ and to share with him the significant role of having fulfilled the figural prophecies of the old law. My examples are all drawn from thirteenth-century Spanish poetry, for it is during that century that one finds the greatest interest in figural interpretation and the greatest activity in the composition of religious literature employing figures.

> Tú María, e yo María,
> Mas non tenemos amas huna via.
> Tu ameste siempre castidat,
> Yo luxuria e malueztad,
> El diablo ffue tu enemigo,
> El fue mi senyor e amigo.
> Tu eres, duenya, mucho omildosa,
> E yo so pobre ergullosa,
> E di mi cuerpo luxuriosa.
> Nuestro Ssenyor amó a ti,
> E pues él amó a tí.
> Duenya, aue merce de mi.

> (vv. 535-46)

In the final years of the twelfth century and the opening decades of the thirteenth, the Franco-Provençal tradition began to exert a growing influence on the literature in the various Spanish dialects.

Along with certain themes, innovations with respect to meters are
also noted, with the traditional Spanish octosyllabic meter yielding
to irregular versification based, it has been suggested, on the in-
complete assimilation of the French metric and stress system. The
Vida de Santa María Egipcíaca is an example both of the influence
of the lives of the saints popular in the Franco-Provençal literatures
and of the metric irregularity characteristic of the borrowings by
the Peninsular poets. [3]

The Spanish version of the well-known legend of the penitent
Mary of Egypt varies in no great detail from other current elabora-
tions. The poet begins with a traditional opening statement concerning the profit to be derived from the "exemplum" which follows, referring to the way in which María's story reminds us of the
all-embracing mercy of God for the repentant sinner. We learn of
the woman's birth in Egypt and how she left her home and family
to seek profit in Alexandria, where she enters a life of sin and degradation. What emerges is a picture of the denizen of Alexandrian
brothels.

One day María observes a boatload of pilgrims embarking for
the Holy Land. She decides to follow, earning her passage in the
time-honored tradition of her profession. It is the month of May,
and the pilgrims arrive in Jerusalem in time for the celebration of
the Feast of the Ascension. María attempts to take part in the
celebration but is barred from entering the church because of her
sinful ways. This abrupt confrontation with her reputation brings
about a sudden realization and sorrow on the part of the sinner.
Beholding an image of the Virgin Mary, she pours forth a confes-

---

3 All quotations are from the *Biblioteca de autores españoles* 57 (Madrid,
1864): 307-18. The numbering of the verses is my own. See A. T. Baker,
"La vie de Sainte Marie l'Egyptienne," *Revue des Langues Romanes* 59
(1916-1917): 145-401; A. M. Monti, *La leggende di Santa Maria Egiziaca
nella letteratura medioevale italiana e spagnola* (Bologna, 1938); A. Mussa-
fia, "Über die Quelle der altspanischen 'Vida de Santa María Egipcíaca,'"
Sitzungsberichte der Kaiserlichen Akademie der Wissenschaften 43 (1863):
153-76. It is interesting to compare our text with another anonymous
treatment of the same subject in Spanish, "Vida de la mujer fuerte, Santa
María Egipcíaca," in Agustín Durán's *Romancero general, Biblioteca de
autores españoles* 16 (Madrid, 1861): 326-28. The way in which the two
versions differ is precisely in the inclusion in our text of the elaboration
which I have called figural. Our text does not differ significantly from the
recent paleographic edition by María S. de Andrés Castellanos (Madrid, 1964).

sion of her sins and pleads for the Holy Mother to intercede on her behalf. A detailed comparison between the two Marys and a retelling of the importance of the passion of Christ in the salvation of mankind follows as part of the woman's lament for her life. She receives God's pardon and is allowed to enter the church. There she hears a voice telling her to cross the River Jordan and enter the desert in search of the Monastery of Sant Iohan, where she will receive Holy Communion. The poem goes on to relate María's wanderings in the desert, the decay of her beauty, and her forty-seven-year search for the monastery. When she finally comes upon it, she is received as a saint come out of the desert. After explaining who she is and the reason for her unusual appearance, she instructs one Fray Gozimás to bring Communion to her on the banks of the River Jordan. The holy man complies with her request, and she leaves him with the intention of returning to the site of their encounter in the desert. Once there she lies down to die and is buried with the aid of a lion; the poet goes on to relate her triumphant entrance into heaven. Meanwhile, the monk has returned to the abbey and, subsequently receiving permission to seek her out again, returns to the desert, finds her body, and gives it burial. Returning to the abbey, Fray Gozimás informs his company among general lamentation of the woman's death. All adopt her as a patron of their prayers and as a model of saintly Christianity.

From this detailed summary of content, the figural structure becomes evident. The focal point of the narrative is the woman's conversion on the occasion of the Feast of the Ascension, in Jerusalem, symbolic in medieval typology of the church triumphant and of earthly perfection. [4] Prior to her conversion, María leads a life of sin in Alexandria. Alexandria is not exactly the sinful Babylon which is the counterpart of Jerusalem, but is more reminiscent of the captivity of the Jewish people before their "salvation" through Moses, one of the most important prefigurements of Christ's salvation of all men. After her conversion, María's wandering in the desert, a real journey in terms of the narrative and not simply an allegorical pilgrimage of the soul, recalls the forty-six days

---

[4] See Johan Chydenius, *The Typological Problem in Dante* (Helsinki, 1958), part 2, "Jerusalem," for a discussion and quotations from medieval sources concerning the typological role of the Holy City.

of the western Lenten season. She receives Communion and salvation in the waters of the River Jordan (another frequent figure in medieval Christian literature and suggestive of the waters of the baptism of Christ and the symbolic baptism of all mankind) during the forty-seventh day of the season. Thus the analogy between María's life, her repentance, and her salvation and assumption by the angels, and hell, purgatory, and heaven, appears to be the central motif of the poem.

María's penance in the desert parallels the temptation of Christ (Matthew 4: 1-11), where he is sent into the desert by the Spirit. After forty days and forty nights of hunger, Christ is tempted by the devil. María's wanderings are equivalent to the forty-six days of Lent, but her story in other respects corresponds to that of Christ: her coming out of Egypt, like Christ's—who in turn thus fulfilled the figure of Moses and the exodus of the children of Israel from bondage in Egypt—and her journey into Jerusalem, her wanderings in the desert, her hunger and temptation by the devil, which she resists with the aid of the Lord and the cloak of grace provided mankind by his passion (vv. 700-93). Finally, María's baptism in the waters of the River Jordan by the Monastery of Sant Iohan and her burial with the aid of the lion complete the parallel drawn by the poet between María's story of sin and redemption and the passion. [5]

María is very much a new Adam. Christ fulfilled the figure of Adam the father of man by offering mankind the means for the redemption of the soul. Yet, in the sense that the world still bears the stain of original sin and will bear it until the Last Judgment, the figure of Adam as the epitome of mankind still has considerable meaning. It is María who realizes the way open to man through Christianity and who, in so realizing, parallels in her life the trajectory of the passion of Christ that had fulfilled the prophecy inherent in the Adam of the Old Law. However, on yet another, more specific level, the intricate relationship which the poet establishes between the prostitute María, the figure of mankind, and the Virgin Mary,

---

[5] The lion came to be the symbol of Saint Mary of Egypt. In addition, legendary natural history had it that lions were born dead, but came to life after three days when breathed upon by their sires. Thus the lion has become also a traditional symbol of the resurrection of Christ.

the Mother of God, is an elaboration in terms of one central detail of the basic figural structure of the work.

In the first part of the narrative, the reader is treated to an extensive description of María's sinful past. The poet's description, based on an abundant use of topoi, sketches for the reader a picture of a beautiful woman, fit for a king:

> De aquell tiempo que ffue ella
> Después no nasçio tan bella
> Nin reyna nin condessa
> Non viestes tal como esta...
>
> (vv. 210-13)

This "queenly figure" of the sinful world of illicit pleasure is displaying her beauty one morning in May when she comes upon the boat carrying the pilgrims to Jerusalem (vv. 262-74). The contrast between the Babylonian Alexandria and the City of God, Jerusalem, is a fundamental point of departure for the work. May is the month devoted to the Virgin Mary. [6] May is also the month during

---

[6] Note Alfonso's (unnumbered) *cantiga* on the figural nature of May, "Ben vennas, Mayo, et con alegría." The composition is primarily interesting for its structure. The poet begins each stanza with an apostrophe to May. When read alone and together these first lines form a sort of litany of joys on the festive month when nature and the flesh come alive again after the forced abstinence of winter. The fourteen pleasures of May are a typical pagan encomium and represent commonplaces from the poetry on the theme. The joyful nature of the reawakening of the world and the senses is reinforced by the *zéjel*-refrain "Ben vennas, Mayo, et con alegría," a frequent poetic device in Spanish medieval poetry, an inheritance from the Arabian literature, and a permanent fixture in Alfonso's poetry. Between the first lines, reminiscent of abandoned delights, and the recurring *estribillo,* the poet dwells upon the principal concern of his *cantiga,* praises of and petitions to the Virgin Mary, both for her own qualities and for her intercession with her son. Two things are striking here: the juxtaposition of the Marian praises with the pagan encomium of May, and the lack of a direct and well-wrought connection between the first lines of the stanzas on the one hand and the second, third, and fourth lines on the other. For example, in the eleventh stanza, we would expect a very clear relationship between the "Ben vennas, Mayo, con pan et con vino" and the following verses; yet the connection is slight if not impertinent, and the poet seems to lose the opportunity to refer to the sacrifice of the mass. See David William Foster, "Medieval Poetic Tradition in Two *Cantigas* by Alfonso el Sabio," *Romance Notes* 8 (1967): 297-304. In passing see Eugenio Asensio, "Las canciones de mayo," in his *Poética y realidad en el cancionero peninsular de la edad media* (Madrid, 1957), pp. 37-42.

which the Feast of the Ascension usually occurs, and the pilgrims
that María joins have planned to be in Jerusalem for the ceremonies
commemorating that holy day. Thus both the geographical and the
temporal focal points of the poem are significant typological symbols.

María joins the pilgrimage to Jerusalem, but remains the wicked
among the penitent:

> Mas non era aquella noche
> Que el diablo con ella non fuesse;
> Bien la cuydaua enganyar
> Que ella pereçiesse en la mar;
> Mas non le fizo nengun tuerto
> que Dios la sacó a puerto.
> Quando ffue arribada
> Dolienta fue e deserrada;
> Lorando seye en la marina,
> Non ssabe ques faga la mesquina; ...
> E llorosa e desconsseiada
> En Iherusalem entraua;
> Mas non dexó hi de pecar
> Ante començó de peorar;
> Agora oyt qual perdiçion,
> Antes de la Açenssion;
> Ella fue tan peyorada,
> Meior le fuera non fues nada.
>
> (vv. 395-420)

Although the poet does not make specific reference to the fact
at this point, Jerusalem, both the City of God and the earthly church,
admits the unrepentant as well as the repentant. The Church of the
present Christian Law survives in the face of the worldly sins of
the flesh, which have their embodiment in María Egipcíaca. It is
only after the Last Judgment that sin will be definitively defeated
and the eschatological Jerusalem established for all eternity. In the
expectation of this event, the Christian living in the sinful world of
the present undertakes the pilgrimage to Jerusalem as a prefigurement of his attainment of the heavenly city to come. At every step
of the way he encounters the agents of the devil, the Marías, to
distract him from his goal:

> El dia vino de la Asçenssion,
> Alli ffue grant proçession,

De los pelegrinos de vltra-mar
Quen van a Dios a rogar,
Los buenos omnes e los romeros,
Al templo van a rogar a Deus,
Non sse perçibió María,
Menosse entrellos en companya.
Menosse entrellos en proçession
Mas non por buena entençion.
Los pelegrinos quando la veyen
Ssu coraçon non ge lo ssabien,
Que si ellos ssopiessen quien era María
Non aurien con ella companyia.

(vv. 424-37)

María is denied physical entrance to the church because of her sins. In one of the frequent allegorical devices to be found in figural works, her entrance is prevented by a party of armed men (vv. 441-51). In a figurative sense, María's sins stand between her and the salvation of the soul represented by the Church in its broader sense.

In an abrupt change of heart, María repents her life of degradation. Her conversion is perhaps too brusque to satisfy the reader searching for a psychological justification for the actions of the sinner. However, the poet is not concerned with psychological motives, but with the interplay of the figural concepts of sin and redemption which he is manipulating in his narrative:

Quando vió que non podie auer la entrada
Atrás faze la tornada;
Alli esta muy desmayada,
A vn requexo es assentada.
Aqui comiença a pensar
E de coraçon llorar...

(vv. 452-57)

María sees an image of the Virgin Mary and begins the long lament leading to her absolution by God and injunction to do penance in the desert. Her lament is characterized by an acknowledgement of her sinful past, a praise of the Mother of God, and, most important to the figural structure of the work, a recounting of the passion of Christ:

Quando [Dios] le echó [a Adam] de parayso,
Por la mançana que en boca miso,

Assí cuydó fer al tu fiio
Mas mucho fue ende repiso.
E por tres vezes le ensayó,
Mas nada non ende leuó.
E quandol vió armada tan fuerte
Por trayçion le buscó muerte.
Mucho fue la muerte bien aurada,
Por-que fue restaurada,
E ssi él non muriesse
Non es homne que parayso houiesse. ...
Del infierno quebrantó las çerraduras
E todas las enclauaduras;
Pues sacó a los que bien querie
Que el diablo dentro tenie.
Fuera sacó los sus amigos,
Que el diablo dentro tenie catiuos.
Sacólos dende por grant oso ...
A los varones apareçió,
Con ellos XL dias moró;
La ley nueua les mostró,
En la boca los besó,
Condonolos con ssu dulçe madre,
Subiósse al çielo al ssu padre.

                                    (vv. 558-89)

This passage reveals several important figural topoi. The first is the belief that Christ established a New Law, a new order of the universe, which will serve as the basis for the Last Judgment, when the eternal order will be instituted. The poet also makes reference to the necessary passion and redemption of Christ, necessary in the sense that it is the only means of saving mankind. It may be theologically radical to assert that the sinful nature of man demands the passion of Christ. Nevertheless, within the framework of the figural order, it more or less follows as a natural result of the fall of man, without the poet, often possessing less than a learned School-man's erudition, being aware of the more subtle pattern of prefigure-ment and fulfillment developed by the theoretical treatises.

The poet in this passage, through María's plea for intercession, refers to the role played by the Virgin Mother. Today we tend to conceive popularly of Mary as having attained her final position in heaven beside her divine son. However, the medieval poet is quite

explicit in seeing a place for the Virgin Mother which will come as
a result of the fulfillment of the prophecy of the Last Judgment:

> Quando verna al jutgamiento,
> Que jutgará todo este ssieglo,
> Tu serás mucho honrrada
> Como duenya tan preçiada.

(vv. 596-99)

Her petition ended, María returns to the church free from the
stain of sin. There she hears the voice sending her into the desert
to carry out her penance. She is to seek the Monastery of Sant
Iohan on the banks of the River Jordan. The poet's figural geography
is obvious here: in addition to the City of God, Jerusalem, María is
to make the Communion in the presence of the river in which
St. John the Baptist baptized Christ.

The poet describes María's penance in the desert at great length.
The desert hermit is a frequent topos of medieval religious poetry,
and the poets dwell at length upon the privation ("Despues andido
quarenta annyos / Desnuda e ssin panyos," vv. 700-701), torments
("Quando huna espina la firia / Vno de sus pecados perdia," vv.
752-53), and temptations ("El diablo la quiso tentar. / E todo lo
quisiera remembrar / Lo que ella ssolia amar," vv. 781-83) which
the sinner must undergo before being cleansed of his sins. In the
case of María, she must wander forty-seven years, one year for each
day of Lent, before attaining her own redemption on the forty-
seventh day, corresponding to Easter and the redemption of all
mankind. Before receiving the Holy Eucharist, Fray Gozimás
questions her on the meaning of the Christian sacrifice, and her
reply effectively summarizes the meaning for Everyman of Lent, the
sacrifice of the mass, and Easter:

> Duenya, dixo de plan:
> Esto sepas que es pan.
> Es cuerpo de Ihesu-Christo
> Que por nos priso martirio.
> E priso muerte e pasion,
> E dionos grant saluaçion.
> Creyes esto, amiga mia?
> Bien lo creyo, dixo María.
> Por la grant culpa que Adam fizo,

> Por la mançana que misso,
> Aquesta sangre nos a él dada
> Loco es qui la tiene en nada.
> El ge lo dió, ella lo reçibió.
> La carne çomió e la sangre beuió.
>
> (vv. 1254-67)

Her redemption complete, María prays to the Virgin for death, and in a state of grace, returns to the desert and dies. Her death and immediate reception into the ranks of the chosen, thus bypassing purgatory, not only reinforce the portrayal of her saintliness but reaffirm as well the extent to which the typology of the poem is essentially eschatological in nature. María's penance in the desert is the purgatory of Everyman, and the thorough expiation of his sins will culminate in a glorious reception into heaven. In his elaboration of the figural structure of his poem, the anonymous poet has recourse to one specific human figure: the equivalence between María Egipcíaca and the Virgin Mary. On an elementary level, the one is the prostitute and the other the Virgin Mother of God, one the "reina de las rameras" and the other the Queen of Heaven.

Other references are the use of the name María and the importance of May ("En el mes de mayo hun dia / Leuantósse *essa* María," vv. 262-63, italics mine). María Egipcíaca recalls the Virgin's earthly origins and ultimate glorification in her virginity. The sinner's insistence upon the Virgin's human form is a point of reference for the way in which the rose of redemption will flower from the thorns of her sins:

> Grant marauilla fue del padre
> Que su fija fizo madre;
> E fue marauillosa cosa
> Que de la espina sallió la rosa.
> Et de la rosa ssallió friçió,
> Porque todo el mundo saluó.
> Virgo, reyna, creyo por tí
> Que si al tu fiio rogares por mí,
> Si tu pides aqueste don
> Bien ssé que hauré perdon.
> Si tu con tu fijo me apagas
> Bien sanaré de aquestas plagas.
> Virgo, por quien tantas marauillas sson,
> Acába-me este perdon.

Virgo, en post partum virgo,
Acábame amor de tu fiio.
(vv. 513-32)

In the mind of the poet, Santa María Egipcíaca has assumed a role analogous to her virginal counterpart. I have already quoted the lines referring to her reception by the angels into heaven; it is, quite literally, the assumption reenacted. Finally, the monks of the abbey of Sant Iohan accept her as a new and special intercessor before Christ:

Mucho emendaron de su vida
Por enxemplo desta María.
E nos mismos nos enmendemos
Que mucho mester lo auemos.
E roguemos a esta María
Cada noche e cada día.
Que ella ruegue al Criador
Con quien ella houo grant amor.
(vv. 1431-38)

In reviewing the nature of the central figure in the *Vida de Santa María Egipcíaca,* one is struck by the multiple facets of María's personality. [7] She appears now as a figure of Christ, now as a figure of the Virgin Mother. The Spanish version is not unique in comparing Mary of Egypt with Christ. The Italian version adheres closely to those events in the Spanish text which are most reminiscent of the parallel with Christ. [8] The Spanish poet, nevertheless, does appear to be making an essentially unusual departure in this seeming ambivalence in assigning María to Jesus or to his Mother. However, in reality from one point of view such an ambivalence is not absurd: Christ, being the figure of the New Adam, encompassed

---

[7] In his work on Spanish allegory, C. R. Post, *Medieval Spanish Allegory* (Cambridge, Mass., 1915), mentions the *Vida de Santa María Egipcíaca* in passing (p. 23) as one example of the many Spanish works based on French models, thereby supporting his thesis that the French influence on the development of Spanish allegory was considerable and decisive (chapter 3, "The French Influence"). Here, as elsewhere, it is a question of what events the term *allegory* is to be applied to. In this case, Post does not elaborate on his passing reference to this particular work.

[8] See David William Foster, "*De Maria Egypciaca* and the Medieval Figural Tradition," *Italica* 44 (June, 1967): 135-43.

all mankind, the Virgin included. María, as a figure of Christ, is able to recall the passion of the Son of Man inasmuch as she is a generalization of the sinful nature of Adam—of mankind—and of redemption through the sacrifice of the Savior. On a more specific level, as a figure of the Virgin Mother, María's life recalls how an emulation and a fulfillment of the life of the most holy of women can lead the soul to salvation. Through an interaction of the symbolism on these two levels, the general and the specific, María's figural personality is subsequently given greater depth by the poet.

From another point of view, María's dual role reveals a not infrequent tension in popular medieval figural poetry. In bringing Christ into the world, does not Mary precede her son in importance as the founder of the New Law? Theologically, Mary is but another means which God has used to realize his universal plan. However, the poets of the popular Marian literature, in exalting the Virginal Queen, lose sight of Mary's less impressive role in dogmatic teaching and speak of her in terms which challenge those reserved for Christ. The result is often a work which heeds the importance of Christ in the history of mankind, but which puts Mary on a par with her son, implying her equality in importance as a figure. The Spanish *Vida de Santa María Egipcíaca* reveals to a certain degree this equivalence between Christ and Mary. Gonzalo de Berceo, Spain's most devoted follower of the cult of Mary, maintains in several of his works the figural importance of the Virgin. Particular attention is due the introduction to the *Milagros de Nuestra Señora* and the lesser known *Loores de Nuestra Señora*. [9]

> "Gozo ayas, Maria, que el angel credist,
> Gozo ayas, Maria, que virgo conçebist,
> Gozo ayas, Maria, que a Cristo parist:
> La lei vieia çerresti, e la nueva abrist."
>
> (*Milagros*, s. 119)

---

[9] Cf. the following stanza from the *Loores:*

> Maria la egiptiana peccadora sin mesura
> Fue reconçiliada ante la tu figura:
> En ti trovó conseio de toda su rencura,
> Tu li subreleveste toda su fiadura.
>
> (edition cited below, s. 201)

Static Hellenistic allegory and progressive figural interpretation are in general practice mutually exclusive. However, an excellent example of their use together in one poetic context is to be found in Berceo's introduction to the *Milagros de Nuestra Señora*. [10] Berceo divides his introductory stanzas into two parts: stanzas 1-15, containing an exordium and an allegorical *locus amoenus,* and stanzas 16-47, the *glosa* of the allegory. The gloss presents no particular problems of interpretation, and Berceo relies principally upon the tradition of patristic exegesis in both his allegorical figures and in his explication of them. He begins with a prefatory statement reminiscent of the procedures of scriptural interpretation:

> Sennores e amigos, lo que dicho avemos,
> Palabra es oscura, esponerla queremos:
> Tolgamos la corteza, al meollo entremos,
> Prendemos lo de dentro, lo de fuera dessemos.
>
> (s. 16)

In his exposition of the meaning of some fairly common Christian symbols appearing in the first fifteen stanzas of the introduction, Berceo makes it clear that in each case the general symbol has a specific reference to the Virgin. Thus, the poet establishes carefully the point of departure for his narratives and justifies in part his dominant interest in the Virgin as a figure who recalls all the hope and solace of Christianity.

The allegory proper of his work is to be found in the first fifteen stanzas. In terms strictly of poetic rhetoric, it is an extensively developed *locus amoenus* populated by allegorical forms. [11] The *prado*

---

[10] My text is the edition by A. G. Solalinde (Madrid, 1934). Two studies have been devoted to the introduction; neither is particularly adequate in giving more than a commentary: Agustín del Campo, "La técnica alegórica en la introducción de los 'Milagros de Nuestra Señora,' " *Revista de filología española* 28 (1944): 15-57; and Carlos Foresti Serrano, "Sobre la Introducción en los 'Milagros de Nuestra Señora' de Gonzalo de Berceo," *Anales de la Universidad de Chile* nos. 107-108 (1957): 361-67. See Emilio Salcedo, "Berceo en el paraíso" *Ínsula* no. 171 (1961): 10; and Erika Lorenz, "Berceo der 'Naive,' Über die *Einleitung zu den Milagros de Nuestra Señora,*" *Romanistisches Jahrbuch* 14 (1963): 255-68.

[11] See Ernst Robert Curtius, *European Literature and the Latin Middle Ages,* trans. Willard R. Trask (New York, 1953), p. 202. Curtius has been taken to task for his identification of topoi in Berceo's *Milagros* by Dámaso Alonso, "Berceo y los 'topoi,' " in his *De los siglos oscuros al de oro*

which the poet presents, the *aves, fuentes,* and *árboles* are no more
than the veiled metaphors of the rhetorical tradition of Hellenistic
allegory. [12] It is clear in Berceo's mind that the forms which he
advances in the first fifteen stanzas in themselves have no immediate
meaning. In describing them to us, the poet is indulging in an
artistic exercise in which the elements are to be appreciated for
their appropriateness in the context of the *locus amoenus.* On one
very basic level, the *prado* of the introduction is appealing. The poet
demonstrates a certain technical polish in formulating a design of
well-chosen allegorical images. It is only when the poet turns to the
glosa that he concerns himself with infusing his allegory with a
meaning beyond what is patently apparent to an educated Christian.
In explaining the meaning of the first fifteen stanzas, Berceo ceases
to express any interest in the autonomy of his allegory as a poetic
unit. One stanza from the *locus amoenus* and its corresponding gloss
will illustrate the poet's procedure:

> Avie hi grand abondo de buenas arboledas,
> Milagranos e figueras, peros y mazanedas,
> E muchas otras fructas de diversas monedas;
> Mas non avie ningunas podridas nin azedas.
>
> (s. 4)

> Los arbores que facen sombra dulz e donosa,
> Son los santos miraclos que faz la Gloriosa,
> Ca son mucho más dulzes que azucar sabrosa,
> La que dan al enfermo en la cuita raviosa.
>
> (s. 25)

Taking into consideration their content from a literal point of view,
one may observe that the first fifteen stanzas constitute an allegorical
unity within the Hellenistic tradition which the poet comments and
explains for our appreciation and wonderment in the concluding
stanzas of the introduction. The reader is meant to turn immediate-

---

(Madrid, 1958), pp. 139-49. In any event, in terms of its religious significance,
Berceo's *locus amoenus,* with its profane elements (such as the *collige flores*
topos of s. 24) may be considered an example of the *literatura divinizada*
or *a lo divino.* See the interesting study on the subject by Bruce Wardropper,
Historia de la poesía a lo divino en la Cristiandad occidental (Madrid,
1958).

[12] See Post's discussion of Berceo's allegory, pp. 118-28.

ly from the *glosa* establishing the magnificence of the Virgin to the succeeding twenty-five miracles attributed to her.

However, an additional function of the introductory allegory is more than implied. The concluding stanza of the allegory summarizes the effect of the *prado* by assuring the reader that:

> El fructo de los arbores era dulz e sabrido,
> Si don Adam oviesse de tal fructo comido,
> De tan mala manera non serie decibido,
> Nin tomarien tal danno Eva ni so marido.
>
> (s. 15)

Of all the stanzas preceding the *glosa,* this one especially moves the reader to formulate analogies and explanations for himself regarding the meaning of what he has just been told. There are several sets of comparisons emphatically implied by the poet. One deals with the relationship between Adam and the "Yo maestro Goncalvo de Verceo," who is wise enough to avail himself of the comforts of the setting. In more extensive terms, the reader is naturally going to draw a parallel between the *prado* and its delights and the Garden of Eden which man lost through the sin of Adam. Indeed, the poet's words force such a parallel upon us, although it is not expressed in direct terms. Clearly, any such parallel would be figural in nature. Man lost the Garden of Eden through the indiscretions of the father of man; the *prado* which Berceo depicts for us appears to be a lasting fulfillment of the promise indicated by the Old Testament Eden. The figural relationship is drawn in further detail with the reference to the *fructo*; the apple of Eden wrought man's fall, while that of this pleasing meadow offers the security of his salvation. [13] In retrospect, the reader understands the allegorical elements of the introductory stanzas in terms of a figural relationship between the Garden of Eden and Berceo's *prado,* the type and the antitype.

---

[13] For a later figural comparison between the tree—the "source" of the apple of the fall—and the cross—the "source" of the redemption—see J. P. W. Crawford, *"Auto de la quinta angustia que Nuestra Señora passo al pie de la Cruz," Romanic Review* 3 (1912): 280-300. This is an "adoración de la cruz" *auto,* and in vv. 542-76, the poet elaborates the comparison between the cross, the "árbol de fructo precioso", and the antitypical tree of Adam, "aquel árbol profano." See the explicit figural commentary on the "trees" in the Preface (of the Holy Cross) to the mass for Monday of Passion Week.

Such an understanding does not destroy the autonomy of the allegory as a rhetorical *locus amoenus,* and Berceo is not the first in the figural tradition to use Hellenistic allegory in conjunction with typology.

Marginally, the comparison between Adam and the poet may be extended to include the common and popular relationship seen between Eve and the Virgin Mary. Berceo's poem does not dwell on this possibility in any demonstrable way, in part for reasons which have to do with his allegorical meaning of the *prado.*

Figural significance is not confined to the first fifteen stanzas of the introduction. In the *glosa,* Berceo explains the significance of the various delights of his *locus amoenus.* In so doing, he makes several allusions to Old Testament persons usually interpreted by Christianity as prefigurements of Christ. For Berceo, their significance lies in their pertinency to the Virgin:

> El rosennor que canta por fina maestria
> Siquiere la calandria que faz grand melodia,
> Mucho cantó meior el varon Ysaya,
> E los otros prophetas, onrrada conpania.
>
> (s. 28)

> Ella es vollocino que fué de Gideón,
> En qui vino la pluvia, una grand vission:
> Ella es dicha fonda de David el varon,
> Con la qual confondió al gigant tan fellon.
>
> (s. 34)

> El fust de Moyses enna mano portava
> Que confonidió los sabios que Faraon preciava,
> El que abrió los mares e depues los cerrava
> Si non a la Gloriosa, al non significava.
>
> Si metieremos mientes en ell otro baston
> Que partió la contienda que fue por Aaron,
> Al non significava, como diz la lection,
> Si non a la Gloriosa, esto bien con razon.
>
> (ss. 40-41)

Leaving aside the theological problems raised by Berceo's ingenious interpretations of the Old Testament, it is evident that the Virgin of the *Milagros* has become the center of the Christian drama. [14] It would be natural to assume that the *prado* represents Christianity and the idyllic delights the means for the salvation of mankind. While the latter is true, the poet is unmistakable in his identification of the significance of the setting:

> En esta romeria [de la vida] avemos un buen prado,
> En qui trova repaire tot romeo cansado,
> La Virgin Gloriosa, madre del buen criado,
> Del qual otro ninguno egual non fué trobado,

> Esti prado fué siempre verde en onestat,
> Ca nunca ovo macula la su virginidat,
> Post partum et in partu fue Virgin de verdat,
> Illesa, in corrupta en su entegredat.

(ss. 19-20)

Therefore, the Garden of Eden is fulfilled, not by the Gethsemane of the exegetical figural tradition, but by the Virgin. This concept is basic to Berceo's consideration of the Holy Mother, and it is only incidental that he portrays her in terms of an allegorical *locus amoenus* clarified by a detailed *glosa*.

With respect to the basic meaning of the Virgin in Berceo's introduction, it seems apparent that he conceives of her within the figural concept of the history of mankind, and he takes pains to demonstrate that it is she who constitutes for man the most effective means of his salvation. It is for this reason that the poet allows himself such a radical departure from what we would accept as orthodox Christianity. Certainly, even in the medieval popular cult of Mary, the idea that the Virgin was the fulfillment of the types of Eden, Isaiah, Gideon's fleece, Moses, and Aaron's rod could not have been common practice, either theologically or

---

[14] See also Berceo's opinions concerning the inspiration of the New Testament:

> Las quatro fuentes claras que del prado manavan,
> Los quatro evangelios esso significavan,
> Ca los evangelistas quatro que los dictavan,
> Quando los escrivien, con ella se fablaban.

> Quatro escrivien ellos, ella lo emendava,
> Esso era bien firme, lo que ella laudava:
> Pareze que el riego todo della manava,
> Quando a menos della nada non se quiava.

(ss. 21-22)

poetically. Berceo's typology is uniquely his own and reveals more than anything else the extent of his devotion and allegiance to the Virgin.

The opening stanzas of the introduction have often been taken as one of the many charming personal notes of the work.[15] The poet addresses his audience:

> Amigos e vasallos de Dios omnipotent,
> Si vos me escuchassedes por vuestro consiment,
> Querria vos contar un buen aveniment,
> Terrédeslo en cabo por bueno verament.
>
> Yo maestro Gonçalvo de Verçeo nomnado
> Iendo en romeria caeçí en un prado
> Verde e bien sençido, de flores bien poblado,
> Logar cobdiçiaduero por omne cansado.
>
> (ss. 1-2)

Even if it were not for the explanatory *glosa* and the clarification that *romeria* here means life (ss. 17-18), it would be inevitable that the reader understand these lines poetically rather than empirically or autobiographically. Berceo is using here the topos of the *homo viator,* man as a voyager on the pilgrimage of life. It is a topos dignified by a long line of classical, medieval, and modern writings, and hardly needs further explanation. The elaboration of the topos in terms of an adventure which the poet experiences is more common to medieval literature, and derives from the way in which the medieval artist generally sees himself as a figure of

---

[15] The traditional approach to Berceo as a poet who makes constant references to himself and to his work in a way which is very appealing to the modern reader is reaffirmed in a recent full-length study of Berceo's poetry, Joaquín Artiles, *Los recursos literarios de Berceo* (Madrid, 1964), "Presencia de Berceo en su obra," pp. 19-23. Dámaso Alonso, *De los siglos oscuros,* is also concerned with the intense personal note of Berceo's writings and the sincerity of his personal allusions (as opposed to the possibility of many of them being topoi). I see no problem in attributing an immediate, personal meaning as well as a transcendant, figural significance to these first-person references. In terms of the study of the work of art, the critic is more interested in the context of an utterance than he is in its possible autobiographical importance and/or sincerity. One assumes that a work of art is not sincere or insincere, but rather good or bad as determined on the basis of aesthetic criteria: realization of structural design and language.

all mankind. [16] In most instances, whether or not the poet actually undertook the journey or pilgrimage described is immaterial; what is important is that he intends us to believe literally that he did. This is the case with Dante, and it is the case with Berceo, who does not give any further meaning for the *yo* of the second stanza in the *glosa* which gives a higher meaning to everything else. The fact that the *romeria* represents life and the *prado* the Virgin Mary does not alter from a narrative point of view the poet's originally stated relationship to it. Within the figural frame of reference the literal reality of his *romeria* remains firmly established.

Beyond the introduction, Berceo's *Milagros de Nuestra Señora* do not demonstrate a reliance on the figural interpretation. [17] In part, this is a result of the poet's principal interest in discussing the relevancy of the Virgin to the wayward man of the here and now, rather than her significance in the abstract terms of the history of man. In addition, the validity of the Virgin as an important element in the life of the humble Christian has been, by the end of the introduction, firmly established within the figural scheme of Christianity.

> Tú que lo que perdió á Eva
> Cobraste por quien tú eres,
> Tú, que nos diste la nueva
> De perdurables placeres;
> Tú, bendita en las mugeres,

---

[16] See Leo Spitzer's important article, "Note on the Poetic and Empirical 'I' in Medieval Authors," *Traditio* 4 (1946): 414-22.

[17] There is a reference to a few Old Testament figures in *Milagro* 19, "Un parto maravilloso." *Milagro* 22, "El náufrago salvado," concludes with the following figural topoi:

> Los que por Eva fuemos en perdición caidos,
> Por ella [i.e., la Virgen] recombramos los solares perdidos:
> Si por ella non fuese iazriamos amortidos;
> Mas el so sancto fructo nos ovo redemidos.

> Por el so sancto fructo que ella concibió,
> Que por salud del mundo passion e muert sufrió,
> Issiemos de la foya que Adan nos abrió,
> Quando sobre deviedo del mal muesso mordió.

> (ss. 621-22)

In general, Berceo's *Milagros* rely on a confusion of Mary and Christ, as revealed in the introduction and in the quote from *Milagro* 4, which prefaces my discussion of the introduction.

> Si nos vales,
> Darás fin á nuestros males.
>
> (Juan de Encina, "De nuestra Señora," s. 5)[18]

If Juan del Encina's estimation of the Virgin Mary does not quite attribute to her the means for the salvation of mankind, his poem does reveal that as late as the waning of the Middle Ages, the popular medieval topos of the "Virgen Redentora" was still a valid commonplace. Much earlier Berceo had written his *Loores de Nuestra Señora,* perhaps one of the most audacious examples of the assigning of the major part of the figural role of Christ to the Virgin: [19]

> Madre, tu eres dicha fuente de piadat,
> Tu fuisti reliquiario pleno de sanctidat,
> La tu merçed spera toda la christiandat,
> Ca por ti commo cree, ganara salvedat.
>
> (s. 199)

Although considerably less known than the *Milagros,* the *Loores* is one of Berceo's finest pieces. His poetry is much more versatile than in the several *Vidas,* where it often approaches doggeral under the weight of the poet's extensive catalogue of the miracles performed by the saints whose lives he relates. (After the *Milagros,* the *Vidas* have attracted the most scholarly interest, unfortunately more for extrinsic reasons than anything else.) Berceo divides his work into several smoothly interlocking sections: an encomium to the Virgin, followed immediately by a demonstration of how Mary fulfilled the figural prophecies of the Old Testament (to approximately s. 26). Almost imperceptibly the poet shifts his point of interest to Christ and relates the standard figural aspects of the Savior; references to the Virgin Mother and her relationship to her son are prominent (approximately ss. 27-175). Following the conclusion of his analysis of what man has been promised in God's order yet to come, the poet speaks for all mankind and the plight of the latter in the sinful here and now. He turns to the Virgin and appeals to

---

[18] Quoted in Marcelino Menéndez y Pelayo, *Antología de poetas líricos castellanos (textos y notas),* 2 vols. (Buenos Aires, 1943), 2: 105-106.
[19] My text is from the *Biblioteca de autores españoles* 57 (Madrid, 1864): 93-100.

her mercy, secure in the knowledge that it is her efficacy wherein he should seek salvation (ss. 176-95). The poet addresses the Virgin and prays for her to intercede on behalf of man. He speaks of those whom the Virgin has aided, and concludes by seeing himself—the "poetic I" of mankind—as a new Adam figure, held in Egyptian captivity from which he implores Mary, the redemptive figure, to free him (ss. 196-233):

> Madre merçed te pido por mis atenedores,
> Ruegote por mis amigos que siempre los meiores,
> Resçibi en tu encomienda parentes e sennores,
> En ti nos entregamos todos los pecadores.
>
> Por mi que sobre todos pequé, merçed te pido,
> Torna sobre mi, madre, non me eches en olvido,
> Trayme del peccador do yago embebido,
> Preso so en Egipto, los viçios me an vendido.
>
> (ss. 230-31)

From this analysis it may be seen that Mary is prominent throughout the poem as a figure which fulfills the Old Law quite on the same level of importance as Christ. Although the poet is willing to discuss Christ's role in the history of the redemption of mankind, his ideas on the subject are relatively unoriginal, and the life of Christ is continually related to Mary's. Furthermore, when the poet dwells on the relationship of the humble man to the meaning of Christ's story, it is Mary whom he addresses and upon whom he depends for his salvation. The result is that Christ invested mankind with the potential for his salvation, but it is Mary upon whom man depends for his freedom from sin, the realization of grace, and the attainment of salvation. This all may make for poor theology, but it is the basis of a certain amount of popular medieval Marian literature.

From the outset of the work, Berceo very clearly sees the Virgin as a prominent figure of the prophecies of the Old Testament:

> Patriarchas et profetas todos de ti dissieron,
> Ca por Spiritu Sancto tu virtut entendieron:
> Profeçias e signos todo por ti fiçieron
> Que cobrarian por ti los que en Adan cayeron.
>
> (s. 5)

The new Adam is not the Christ of the more didactic and formal figural exegesis; it is the Virgin Mary's coming to restore man from the fall which the Holy Ghost inspires the prophets to foretell. In the case of Mary of Egypt, the figure of man in the present, and the Adam of today the antitype is both Mary and Christ. Where the anonymous poet fused the son and the mother in one contemporaneous figure, Berceo's Mary is by herself the source of mankind's salvation and the fulfillment of the figure of Adam. The poet goes on to elaborate his exhaltation of the Virgin in a series of stanzas which border on exegesis:

> La mata que paresçio al pastor ençendida
> Et remanesçió sana commo ante tan cumplida,
> A ti significaba que non fuisti corrompida,
> Nin de la firmedumbre del tu voto movida.

> A ti cataba, madre, el signo del baston
> Que partió la comanda que fue pora Aaron:
> Fuste sin rayz e seco adusso criazon,
> Et tu pariste Virgo sin toda lesion.

> En ti se cumplió, sennora, el dicho de Isaya
> Que de radiz de Iesse una verga saldria,
> Et flor qual non fue vista dende se levantaria,
> Spiritu Sancto con VII dones en la flor posaria.

> Madre tu fuisti la verga, el tu fijo la flor,
> Que resuçita los muertos con su suave odor,
> Saludable por vista, vidable por sabor,
> Pleno de los siete dones, solo dellos dador.

> Tu fuiste la cambariella que dize el Psalmista,
> Ende salió el esposo con la fermosa vista,
> Gigante de grandes nuevas que fizo grant conquista,
> Rey fue et obispo et sabidor legista.

> (ss. 6-10)

Berceo has invoked in these introductory stanzas a series of important Old Testament figures which, from a more traditional point of view, have been taken as figures of Christ. These are the same figures which the poet refers to in the introduction to the *Milagros*. At the same time, and I consider this more significant, Berceo combines figures which are acceptably applicable to the Virgin—Isaiah's prophecy of a virgin from the line of Jesse—with a figure such as Aaron's rod, popularly applied to Christ. The poet justifies his practice through references to Mary as the means of mankind's salvation:

> La tu figura, madre, traie el velloçino
> En qui nuevo miraglo por Gedeon avino:
> En essi vino la pluvia, en ti el Rey divino:
> Por vençer la batalla tu abriste el camino.
>
> La puerta bien çerrada que diçe Ezechiel,
> A ti significaba que siempre fuiste fiel:
> Por ti passó sennero el sennor de Israel,
> E desto es testigo el angel Gabriel.
>
> Estos fueron et otros, madre, tus mesageros,
> Muchos ovieron estos de tales companneros,
> De todas gentes fueron, ca non unos senneros,
> Todos en tu materia salieron verdaderos.
>
> (ss. 11-13)

There is less interest in the Old Testament prophecies concerning the Coming of Christ, and greater emphasis is placed on figures, "mesageros," which foretell the Virgin Mother. Although the main body of the poem is devoted to Christ, the narrative is purportedly devoted to Mary. The Virgin is not discussed at length, yet the introductory stanzas make it quite clear that the significance of the son derives from the fulfillment by the mother of the prophecies of the Old Law, that the New Law may be properly said to have its origins in Mary:

> Sancto fue el tu parto, sancto lo que pariste,
> Virgo fuiste ante del parto, virgo remaneçiste,
> Pariendo, menos-cabo ninguno non prisiste:
> El dicho de Isaya en eso lo compliste.
>
> (s. 26)
>
> Madre, en tu parto nuevos signos cuntieron,
> Pastores que velaban nuevas lumbres vidieron,
> La verdat de la cosa nuevos cantos ovieron.
> De gozo e de paz nuevos cantos oyeron.
>
> Otros signos cuntieron assaz de maraviella:
> Olio manó de piedra, nasçio nueva estrella,
> El tiempo fue destruto quando pario la punçella,
> Paz fue por todo el mundo qual non fue ante de ella.
>
> (ss. 28-29)

In addition to assigning to the Virgin Mother the point of departure for the salvation of mankind, Berceo transforms her into a woman who consciously and conscientiously carries out the divine plan:

> Madre, de aqueste passo profetó Malachias
> Commo vernia al templo el amado Mesias;
> Et tu commo sabias leyes e profeçias,
> Tu lo fuisti cumpliendo commo venian los dias.
>
> (s. 34)

Berceo ignores the several biblical passages in which a bewildered Mary does not understand the words "I must be about my Father's business." The Spanish poet raises the object of his enthusiasm to a level of awareness which sees Mary as assuming a principal role in effecting God's mission for his son. Berceo's Virgin is far removed from the uncomplicated and passive Mary of the Bible, and much closer to the active intercessor of man's prayers. The difference in the case of Berceo's narratives is that she plays an active role during Christ's life, while the Mary of the devout is the Mary of the Assumption, the mother who sits at the right hand of her attentive son.

Mary, then, is a *means* for the fulfillment of the figural prophecies. When Berceo turns to the role of Christ, he employs the topoi of the tradition. The poet refers to several of the most important figural fulfillments of Christ. On baptism:

> Quando vino el tiempo de complida edat,
> Reçibió el baptismo con grant humildat,
> Non porque fuesse en elli ninguna suçiedat,
> Mas que prisiese el agua de tal actoridat.
>
> San Ioan el Baptista quandól vio venir,
> Mostróle con su dedo et empezó de decir:
> Aquel cordero debe el mundo redemir,
> Lo que debia él dar, biene de mi a reçebir.
>
> (ss. 43-44)

On the mass:

> Çelebró la gent la Pascha, çenó con sus amigos,
> Fizo decretos nuevos, destaio los antigos,
> Los que tenia por hermanos, salieronle enemigos,
> Cada unos quales fueron los fechos son testigos.

> Estando a la çena fizo su testamiento,
> En el pan, en el vino fizo grant sacramiento,
> Pusonos de su muerte un fuerte remembramiento,
> Desí labó los piedes, dió nuevo mandamiento.
>
> (ss. 56-57)

On the passion:

> Viernes fue aquel dia, siempre será nombrado,
> En tal mesmo dia fue Adan engannado,
> Fue por salvar el mundo Ihu Xpo cruçificado,
> Çerca de él dos ladrones del un el otro lado.
>
> (s. 66)

Berceo describes the passion in detail, and sees it, properly enough, as the culmination of Christ's promise to mankind. The narrative contains more figural references than it would be convenient to quote. Most significant, however, is the poet's shift from a narrative orientation which is discursive and descriptive to a point of view which involves relating the passion of Christ with the poet's life of sin. He sees the redemption in personal terms; [20] he refers again to Mary in such a way as to imply her coequality with Christ in bringing the poet salvation:

> Quanto en todo el mundo podria seer asmado
> Lo que saber podemos et lo que es çelado,
> Todo por esto fue fecho, fuera sea peccado:
> Agora por mis debdos veo a él prendado.

> En grant verguenza yago mezquino peccador,
> Quando veo por mal siervo muerto tan buen sennor,

---

[20] A few stanzas earlier, Berceo refers to the cleansing power of Christ's wound:

> Aun fizo mas la gente descreida,
> En el diestro costado diol una grant ferida,
> Manó ende sangre e agua, salut de nos e vida,
> Por ende sancta Yglesia del muesso fue guarida.
>
> (s. 77)

The reference is either unacceptably anachronistic, or else the poet is employing the term "Yglesia" in a much more general sense than as an institution. Of course, figuralli, the blood and water of Christ are the wine and water of the mass which commemorates the passion. Berceo's point of view here is nonpersonal and abstract, even though his symbols may be more popular than doctrinal.

Yo falsé su mandado, él muere por mi amor.
En grant verguenza yago mezquino peccador.

Sennor bien sé que vives maguer muerto te veo:
Maguer muerto, que vives firme-mente le creo:
Tu mueres que yo viva, en esto firme seo,
La tu resurection yo mucho la deseo.

Todas estas mezquindades que te veo sofrir,
A Isayas creo que las oy deçir:
Quando lloró Iheremias esto vedia venir:
Sennor seas loado porque quisiste morir!

Si tu nunca morieses vivir yo non podria,
Si tu mal non sofrieses yo de bien non sabria,
Si tu non deçendiesses yo nunqua non subria:
Loado seas Xpo, et tu virgo Maria!

(ss. 93-97)

Finally, the poet concludes his account of Christ's life as fulfillment with an analysis of the correspondence between Sunday as
commemorating the completion of the creation of the world and
Sunday as commemorating the completion of Christ's mission in the
resurrection, thus tying together the importance of Sunday in both
the Old and the New Laws (ss. 103-106).

The poet returns to Mary as he describes the visit of the three
women to the tomb on Easter morning. This is *not* the occasion
for reiterating man's salvation through the passion of the new Adam
who has just arisen. Instead, Berceo refers to the role of Mary as
the new Eve:

Si por mugier fuemos e por fuste perdidos,
Por muger e por fuste somos ia redemidos;
Por essos mismos grados que fuemos confondidos,
Somos en los solares antigos revestidos.

Madre, el tu linage mucho es enalzado,
Si Eva falta fizo, tu lo as adobado,
Bien paresçe que don Xpo fue vestro abogado,
Por ti es tu linage, sennora, desreptado.

Alegrate sennora que alegrar te debes,
Ca buenas nuevas corren e nuevo tiempo vedes,
Lo que speresti siempre, sennora, ya vedes,
Alegrate sennora que alegrarte debes.

(ss. 110-12)

Given Berceo's concept of Mary and given the structure of the *Loores*, designed as it is to reiterate the importance and the stature of Mary, it would be unjust to call untimely these praises just quoted. Mary is the point of departure for the poem; Christ is unquestionably secondary to her in emphasis. While the poet does not ignore the more orthodox concept of Christ, in the *Loores* the Son of Man derives his significance and his transcendency from the ever-present Mary, who is assigned the central narrative role in the work. The following sixty stanzas of the poem describe the activities of the apostles, as they go forth to preach the word of Christ, and Berceo details the manner in which they continue the fulfillment of the figural prophecies. Gradually, the poet brings his story of Christianity up to date by referring to himself as the present-day sinner in need of the promise of Christ and the intercession of Mary. In employing the "poetic I," Berceo does more than involve himself personally in his narrative. He stresses the way in which Christ's fulfillment is a progressive activity which embraces the totality of human history. The man of the present is also Adam, a sinner in need of the continual renewal of the Christian story, and a sinner who will eventually have to face the final realization of history in the Last Judgment:

> Toda sancta iglesia aqui ovo comienzo,
> Daquende ovo forma e todo ordenamiento,
> Mas fue tu fijo, madre, piedra de fundamiento,
> Sobre él fue levantado todo el fraguamiento.

> Otro grant privilegio aven estos varones,
> El dia del juiçio juzgarán las razones,
> Ellos con el tu fijo partirán los gualardones,
> Destaiarse an por siempre iamas las petiçiones.
>
> (ss. 168-69)

> Mostrarnos ha don Xpo todas sus feridas,
> Las quales por nos ovo en la cruz resçebidas:
> Todas las negligençias y serán façeridas,
> Serán las elemosinas de los buenos gradidas.
>
> (s. 172)

> Yo common parezré peccador en esse dia,
> Que siempre fiçi e dixi vanidat e folia?

De bien nin dixi nin fiçi un dinero valia,
Mezquino peccador, que faré aquel dia?

(s. 176)

The poet closes with an appeal to the Virgin to intercede on his behalf. The narrative trajectory has moved from a detailed analysis of the Old Testament prophecies concerning the Virgin and the salvation of mankind which she would engender, through a re-telling of Christ's fulfillment of God's plan in his passion and resurrection, along with several additional references to Mary's part in bringing the Savior to mankind, and concludes with a description of the Last Judgment of man and the latter's dependency upon and faith in the Virgin Mother to intercede on his behalf. Thus, in Berceo's concept of figural history, it is Mary who, from the earliest prophecies of the Old Law to the Last Judgment which is yet to come, has given unity to the hopes of mankind for salvation.

The concept of Mary elaborated by Berceo and the anonymous author of the *Vida de Santa María Egipcíaca* is distinctly popular in nature and directed at an audience which would be uninterested in the critical scrutiny of their Virgin from a theological point of view. [21] Although presented within the framework of the figural vision of history and mankind, it would be safe to say that the patristic tradition of scriptural exegesis did not know such a Mary. [22] Even in their most fanciful moments, the formal exegetes were usually able to maintain a restraint and a perspective on the matter which was apparently unduly conservative for the enthusiastic Gonzalo. From an artistic point of view, my contention is that it is useful to understand the popular medieval concept of the Virgin as it is revealed in the works which I have discussed. [23] For the sake

---

[21] Claudio Vilá, "Estudio mariológico de los milagros de Nuestra Señora de Berceo," *Berceo* 8 (1953): 343-60, attempts to reconcile—rather unconvincingly—the unorthodox passages of Berceo's *Milagros* with some finer points of theology.

[22] The same, of course can be said of Dante's Mary-Mediatrix figure, Beatrice, as she is elevated to the role of Christ in the *Paradiso* of the *Divina commedia*.

[23] For a discussion of an example of a fifteenth-century Mary figure *a lo profano*, see David William Foster, "Sonnet XIV of the Marqués de Santillana and the Waning of the Middle Ages," *Hispania* 50 (September, 1967): 442-46.

of examining the unity of these poetic works—and I am assuming that one will agree that there is an interest in discovering the unity which the poet most assuredly intended his work to have—attention is due the way in which the poet conceives of Mary as the central referential point of his narratives. Not to heed the unusual importance which Mary has been assigned is to overlook the increased density of her personality that results from the poet's organization of his work. The figural interpretation of Mary unites the poem, and without such an interpretation the several threads of the poem would otherwise lack coherency. It is in this way that we can explain the role of Christ in the *Vida* or in the *Loores*—a strong link established between Christ and Mary which, although perhaps theologically unjustifiable, is the poet's way of exalting the Virgin. The artistic unity of these several works comes to depend in large part on the skill of the poet in elaborating his figural analogies. [24]

---

[24] Alfred B. Jacob, in his article "The *Razón* as Christian Symbolism," *Hispanic Review* 20 (1952): 282-301, reworked as chapter 5 of his "The *Razón de Amor,* Edition and Evaluation" (Ph.D. diss., University of Pennsylvania, 1955), discusses that enigmatic thirteenth-century composition from the point of view of sacramental symbolism, focusing on the cooperative lady of the first part as the Virgin. Mr. Jacob is not too convinced himself of his interpretation, hedging and cautioning as he goes along. The result is offered as a possible, panallegoric interpretation which lacks cohesive unity.

CONCLUSION

ONE OF THE MOST CHARACTERISTIC FEATURES of medieval Hispanic literature is the unfortunate paucity of texts in three important genres: the epic, the drama, and, for literature in Castilian, the lyric. Much has been written in the attempt to hypothesize the reasons for this paucity, and some success has been achieved in reconstructing the supposed missing works. Aside from the critic's dismay at no longer having these works at his disposal, the significance of such a circumstance for a study of Christian allegory is to make it extremely difficult to pretend that a fair representation of the typology of the subject has been given. In short, we cannot pretend to have presented a history of the topic such as would have been possible in English literature, where more texts are to be found. Nevertheless, the foregoing study, while eschewing the claim to a thorough representation of the literature of the period, has had as its unifying objective the characterization of a dominant structural motif in medieval Hispanic poetry.

The word *structural* has been emphasized over the more immediately obvious word *thematic* for two reasons. In the first place, the "themes" of this study are generally not original with the poet. Indeed, the very artistic impact of this poetry, if one may indulge for a moment in a sociological generality, was to give literary and artistic form to one of the all-pervasive religiocultural beliefs of the age—that of the continuing dynamic validity of synthetic prophecy. While it is true, of course, that we have learned to subscribe in spirit to the doctrine that form and treatment achieve a unique and characteristic modification of thematic *materia prima,* it does not seem unduly rash not to want to see thematic innovation as the special forte of these poets. By the same token, given the well-developed pattern of myths, stories, and beliefs surrounding the Judeo-Christian concept of divine history, any given body of literature is but a weak spokesman for the themes of that tradition. Therefore, it is not surprising that it would be difficult for us to point to works that are impressive for their grasp of the totality of the tradition—the *Divina commedia,* of course, is the outstanding example, and in Hispanic poetry, the *Poema de Fernán González* is the work which comes closest to incorporating the broad, sweeping vision of synthetic prophecy.

From a literary point of view, therefore, I suggest that the greatest value of these works lies in the elaboration of a structural motif, or of a series of structural motifs that together bespeak a major concern and a major contribution of their authors. As I have tried to point out in the discussion of each individual work, this common structural motif, while obviously deriving from a particular set of themes and a particular manner of looking at the universe, manifests itself in the characteristic unity with which the poems are themselves constructed. Thus, a significant feature occupying our attention has been the density and the interest that the poet is able to lend his compositions through the elaboration of sets of references and patterns of narrative as he develops his theme in terms of the practices of Christian allegory. The result, while often less satisfying than orthodox, nonliterary exegesis, can be a remarkably refreshing way of looking at man and his world. This is particularly true of the *Poema de Fernán González,* with its somewhat startling view of Spanish history, or of the *Vida de Judas,* with its notably unorthodox opinions concerning the validity of that figure in the scheme of sin and redemption, or of the *Libro de buen amor,* where the figural motifs contribute to the prevailing analysis of the complex motives of man's moral attitude.

If we consider the characteristics of each of the three groups of works discussed in this study, some interesting conclusions emerge. Clearly, the literature dealing with Marian themes is the most rewarding, in great part for its significant concept of the dominant role of Mary in the affairs of men's souls. Confined almost exclusively to the thirteenth century, when Hispanic literature was just beginning to mature, these works demonstrate a striking unity in theme and in treatment. It is here where the reader can most readily appreciate the poet's ingenuity in bringing together the threads of his narrative under the principles of a motivating literary design.

Conversely, the examples on the figure of Christ are less impressive in revealing an overall picture of theme or treatment. Perhaps this situation is due to the previously mentioned lacunae in the texts—doubtlessly the recovery of the lost miracle and mystery plays would go far toward rounding out the treatment of the Savior during the centuries under consideration. Nevertheless, in terms of what we have to work with, the poetic elaboration of the available material is either routine—cf. the *Auto de los Reyes Magos*—or dramatically hyperbolic, as in the accommodation of Fernán González as a redemptive figure. Yet, the brief Catalan piece on the fateful pieces of silver is satisfying for its employment of figural analogy in order to suggest a new perspective for the subject matter.

Probably the literature with the greatest appeal to the modern reader is that discussed in the chapter on Adam as the figure of man. Certainly, the works mentioned there are among the most complex and elaborate in their working out of their orientations. One runs the New Critics' risk of preferring the more complex literature simply because it is complex—the difficult ambiguities of the *Libro de buen amor,* the balanced, tripartite reiteration of the *Vida de Judas.* Still, the fact that the major thrust of these works is a coherent vision of man is no minor factor in their increased interest for the modern reader. In placing the timeless dilemma of human sin within the framework of an "ordered theory" of universal history, these works are much more "modern" than the *Cantigas* of Alfonso or the artful personifications of Gil Vicente. This is, to be sure, essentially an anachronistic-relativistic observation, but the point cannot be overlooked in attempting to describe the literary and artistic importance attributed to any of the works presented in this study.

While it is perhaps indisputable that not all of the compositions analyzed deserve recognition for their artistic qualities, my main interest has been to discuss the works in terms of understanding their poetic and aesthetic organization. Again, it is for this reason that the construction of a typology of Christian allegory has had only a secondary importance. Rather, if the critic can address himself knowingly and convincingly to the issues of literary rhetoric, he will have done much to give the works in question a uniqueness that exceeds their status in a literary history. Thus, the importance of the titles dealt with here and the significance of the critical perspective within which they have been examined lie in the poet's attempt to give artistic form and meaning to a vision that goes beyond literature and religion—certainly beyond theological truth—to that of an age and a manner of giving broader meaning to the pilgrimage of man.

INDEX

STUDIES IN ROMANCE LANGUAGES